The Art of **Bird Finding**

The Art of **Bird Finding**

PETE DUNNE

STACKPOLE
BOOKS

To Judy Toups—birder, teacher, writer, friend

Published by
STACKPOLE BOOKS
5067 Ritter Road
Mechanicsburg, PA 17055
www.stackpolebooks.com

Printed in the United States of America

10 9 8 7 6 5 4 3 2 1

First edition

Cover design by Tessa J. Sweigert
Photos by Linda Dunne except where otherwise noted

Library of Congress Cataloging-in-Publication Data

Dunne, Pete, 1951–
   The art of bird finding / Pete Dunne.—1st ed.
      p. cm.
   ISBN 978-0-8117-0896-8
   1. Bird watching.   2. Birds—Habitat.   I. Title.
QL677.5.D84 2011
598.072'34—dc22
                                            2011012104

Contents

First Things First

Bird watching is North America's second-largest and fastest-growing outdoor pursuit. It is also one of humankind's most enduring and pervasive occupations. Birds, and our relation to them, have been part of the written history or oral tradition of every culture on the planet since the advent of human society.

You might guess, therefore, that a great deal has been written about birds, and you would be right: hundreds, even thousands, of books dealing with the biology of birds, bird behavior, and bird feeding, and an ever-increasing number treating the subject of bird identification.

I've been guilty of writing one or three of these myself.

But there is one area of bird study for which there seems to be an unaccountable dearth of information—in fact, to the best of my knowledge, no comprehensive treatment. I'm speaking, of course, about the challenge of *finding* birds. I for one find this avocational shortfall *really* weird.

Let's face it. Before you can get down to the business of identifying or studying or just plain *enjoying* a bird, you must first *find* it. Fail in this regard and bird "watching" becomes a hollow exercise. All the thousands of books written on the subject are rendered academic.

"No broad-based books on bird finding?" I'll bet you're shocked. I was. I just assumed that somebody, sometime, had set down the basic elements and special techniques of engaging the billions of birds of approximately ten thousand species that enliven the planet.

But maybe this is precisely why no book on the subject *does* exist. If birds are everywhere, ranging from polar regions to desert landscapes to the open seas to the most heavily populated urban centers, why write a book on how to find them? If they are everywhere, then . . . they're everywhere! Manifest. Omnipresent.

If this is what you think, then one thing seems evident to me. You've never actually tried to find a bird, have you? Numerous they are. Widely distributed, too. But manifest? Uh, uh.

Oh, sure, you've run into birds here and there. Blundered into the odd robin, crow, or sparrow as you've gone about your business. Yes, some bird species are quite common and have adapted well to the habitats our species frequents—cities, towns, suburban yards. It's the other species, the vast majority of bird species, the ones whose habitat and ours are tangential at best, that pose the challenge. You'll discover, if you haven't already, that finding most of the birds on the planet is not just challenging, it can be downright frustrating.

Birds, you see, are not vain. They don't get up every morning yearning to be discovered and admired by the likes of us. They have their own lives, their own agendas, and if you subscribe to the notion that birds were put on this planet to respond to our beck and call, know that someone, apparently, forgot to send birds the memo. At best, they are indifferent to us. More often, they regard humans as something best avoided. And avoiding us is something professional birds are very good at.

But I think there is another reason why a book like this one has taken so long to come along. For the better part of the nineteenth

If finding birds across North America were as easy as, say, finding mockingbirds on the Galapagos Islands, there would be no need for you to read this book (or for me to write it).

century, when the lives of most Americans were tied to the land, seeing and hearing birds were everyday experiences. The song of meadowlarks and the sight of Barn Swallows nesting under the rafters were part of our rural existence. Who needed a book?

Even in the second half of the twentieth century, there were plenty of birds to enjoy and, for many Americans, ample opportunity to enjoy them. In northwestern New Jersey, when I was a kid, the trees around my parents' suburban home sprouted colorful migrants every morning of every May. In winter, the birdseed I squandered my allowance on attracted hordes of Tree Sparrows, "Slate-colored" Juncos, and a host of year-round resident species, too.

To see birds, all I had to do was step into the backyard or take a walk in the neighboring woods and pick my subject.

But that was then and this is now. And now, in twenty-first-century America, the waves of northbound neotropical migrants I knew in my youth have been diminished. By some estimates, the number of birds migrating north across the Gulf of Mexico each spring is now less than half the number that vaulted it back when Rachel Carson wrote *Silent Spring,* in 1962.

The reasons behind the decline are many, and while it is certainly a matter worthy of your concern, more relevant to the subject of bird finding is the impact that reduced bird populations are going to have upon your ability to find and enjoy birds. The fact is, just standing in your backyard or blundering around in the woods are not the successful strategies they once were. In order for you to experience the waves of birds I knew in my youth, you are going to have to catch a special condition (known as a "migratory wave") or a "fallout" (a weather system–spawned deluge of birds) and put yourself in fortune's path by going to a local "migrant trap" (a place where migratory birds are concentrated).

You are going to have to understand the geographic and meteorological conditions that cause birds to be *here* and not *there* and on *this side* of the hedge and not *the other.* You are going to have to take full advantage of opportunities when you find them, and this means using your brain and your understanding of birds and all the things that drive them as much as you use your eyes and ears.

If you've read this far, chances are you are nodding your head yes because you are a bird-watcher, too. You already know how challenging it can be to find birds. And you hope that reading this book will give you a bird-finding edge.

That is my ambition, too. To set down on paper the basic bird-finding skills that every birder needs plus the many tricks of the bird-finding trade I have amassed over my fifty years of birding and tour leading.

It's not complicated. In fact, a great deal of the art of bird finding is applied common sense—rooted in an understanding of birds, their habits, and habitats.

But make no mistake, the art of bird finding encompasses a skill set that takes time to acquire. That's the bad news. The good news is that, as a skill, it can be passed on from experienced birders to those with less experience. This tradition of mentoring is as old as bird study itself.

The process begins with turning the page.

Introduction:

In Search of the Lost Skill Set

We were standing just off the parking lot and just inside the postage-stamp parcel of woods. Mature oaks, hickory, and maple canopy; dogwood and sassafras understory. Pretty lush shrub layer, too, because here in downtown Fort Lee, New Jersey, browsing deer are few.

It was Earth Day—the day set aside to celebrate our planet's biological riches—and as a New Jersey Audubon staff person, I'd been invited to appear on a local TV station to represent Mother Earth to the viewing audience. New Jersey Audubon, founded to protect and foster awareness of New Jersey's natural endowment, has been around for more than 110 years. I, as NJA's director of natural history information, have been on staff for about a third of this.

Part of the broadcast was to be "in-studio," part in the woodlands out back—where I'd assured the producers we would find birds (and not just pigeons): because of the date (late April, so prime migration time), because of the weather (warm with southerly breezes), and because many resident bird species are versatile enough to live, even thrive, in urban enclaves like Fort Lee.

The trick, of course, is finding them.

I don't know whether the producers believed it. Birds? In the brick and mortar heart of Bergen County? Right across the river from Manhattan and sixty seconds, as the pigeon flies, from the George Washington Bridge?

The two-man TV crew certainly didn't have a lot of faith in the endeavor—and why should they? No doubt they'd parked their cars in this lot a thousand times. Never seen a bird, never heard a bird. That was about to change.

While they busied themselves with their camera, I conducted a quick reconnaissance. It's not correct to say I studied the woods because that denotes a concentration of focus and what I was doing was somewhat the opposite.

I wasn't, precisely, looking for birds. Rather, I was letting them disclose their whereabouts to me, and it wasn't long before one of them obliged—attracting my attention first with a series of soft taps then with the slight motion of its head—a movement made conspicuous because in a woodlands unstirred by wind, even the slightest motion catches and holds a hunting eye.

"Got a woodpecker," I announced matter-of-factly. "A downy."

"WHERE?" they demanded in tone and volume that wouldn't have been out of place had I just advised them that I'd found the remains of Jimmy Hoffa.

"There," I directed, pointing. "On the left side of the first large tree. About twenty feet above the ground."

They couldn't find it. Even though their eyesight and hearing were fine. Even though they made a living bringing cameras to bear on targeted objects.

The bird was in plain view, less than sixty feet away and completely unconcerned about our presence. As a resident species, the woodpecker saw people every day. It had grown used to their oblivious nature, so, indifferent to our presence, it continued to tap away at the tree.

I repeated the directions. Adding that what they were looking for was a small, black and white, salt-shaker-sized bird clinging to the trunk.

They still couldn't find it. They had no search image to call up. Their eyes weren't skilled at sifting through a three-dimensional woodland maze for small birds. And perhaps most of all, their sense of awareness was hobbled by disuse. Even if their eyes did pick up the bird's slight motion (and it's certain they did) and their ears detected the tapping sound (which was perfectly evident) their brains didn't register the significance of these clues. So I elucidated.

"Never mind the bird. Just watch for motion. You're hot-wired to clue in on motion."

That did it. First one then the other located the woodpecker, and then both of them spun and stared, open mouthed, at me.

Downy Woodpeckers are common and widespread, but that doesn't guarantee that they are going to be seen.

"HOW'DYOUSEETHAT?" they demanded. Their expressions of astonishment would not have been out of place if I'd just produced a unicorn.

"I do this for a living," I pointed out. "White-breasted Nuthatch," I added.

"WHERE?" they demanded, again.

"Just went around the back of the same tree. Wait. It'll swing back into view again." And it did. But of course, initially, they had trouble finding this bird, too.

"HOW'DYOUSEETHAT?" they demanded, again. This time they looked at me like I was in league with the devil, practicing some dark art . . . which, it could be argued, I was.

The art of discernment and awareness. These qualities aren't exactly fruit hanging from the tree of knowledge. But they help you find that fruit.

Before I could reply, to tell them that I'd seen the bird fly in and land, I heard a rustling in the leaves. The kind of sound a bird of the forest floor might make while searching for food in the leaf litter.

"White-throated Sparrow," I announced, directing their attention this time to the cryptically colored bird that was busily engaged in the business of foraging among the leaves.

If they were astonished before, they were incredulous now—simply could not comprehend how a person could find a leaf-colored bird crouched among the leaves. And yes, it is tricky. Leaf-colored birds look the way they do specifically to avoid detection.

But that doesn't make them invisible. And the act of scratching through leaf litter produces movement and sound—two of the basic building blocks of human perception.

Of course, you need to be attuned to such things—as my friends in the camera crew clearly were not. They are not alone in this regard. In fact, in twenty-first-century America, most people's bird-finding skills wouldn't do credit to a day-old duckling.

In a little over an hour, we pried a dozen bird species out of that tiny woodlot smack in the middle of Fort Lee. And while the two guys in the camera crew thought it was about the most amazing display they'd ever witnessed, I have to confess that any modestly competent birder could have done it.

So, for that matter, can you. That is the whole point of this book.

1 | Hot-wired for Birds

Whether you know it or not, you are a bird-finding machine. Under the shell of your modern veneer, stripped down to raw sensory receptors, you, Mr. and Ms. *Homo sapiens*, are genetically hot-wired to pick up the clues that say: LOOK, LOOK. BIRD HERE.

Locating birds is largely a matter of letting your eyes and ears do what they are designed to do—sift through the world around you for visual and auditory clues and feed them to the brain—and then disciplining your brain to pay attention to the bird-related data it is getting. Not surprisingly, a discussion relating to boosting your situational awareness constitutes the first part of this book.

Actively *finding* birds—that is, using your understanding of bird behavior to locate birds—is a different discipline. It will command the balance of this book (and, with luck, the rest of your long and happy bird-finding life).

But getting back to the subject, the essence of locating birds is detection, and the tools

Know it or not, you are a bird-finding machine.

we humans bring to bear are our eyes and our ears. The *ability* of these sensory organs to accomplish this task has been honed by evolution. Their *capacity* to do this was pretty nearly complete by the time you left the crib.

Then, through neglect and misuse, you allowed this incredible bird-finding sensory package to be stored in mothballs and gather dust. If you are serious about finding birds, it's time to unpack your visual and auditory tool kit and shake off the dust.

About Ability

Congratulations. If you are reading these words you come from a long line of survivors. Most creatures don't live long enough to breed, but every single one of your ancestors managed this feat. Yes, part of it was luck. But in the case of our species, a key component of our evolutionary survival plan is acute situational awareness.

In nature—and in birding—detection is nine-tenths of the law. Here, impala and birders bring their senses to bear on their surroundings.

The first step in avoiding danger is recognizing it. For thousands of generations, humans and protohumans have relied upon eyes and ears to warn of approaching threats. An abrupt movement in the underbrush could be a lion tensing its muscles for a charge, but your ancestor's eyes were refined to pick up this subtle motion, and this trait was passed on to you.

A snapping branch may warn of an enemy's approach. But the ears of your ancestors were not only attuned to the sound but able to pinpoint its source then guide this critical intelligence to your brain for rapid analysis and response. This auditory-detection package was passed on to you, too.

We have other senses: taste, feel, and smell. But while these may serve a self-preservation function, they have only limited application in the bird-watching arena. Except for locating penguin colonies (whose rancid shrimp odor can be detected miles from land) and Great Horned Owls (whose partiality to skunks makes them pretty pungent), our human sense of smell is rarely used to locate birds.

Back to eyes and ears.

The Eyes Have It

Have you ever wondered how eyes do what they do: distinguish colors, perceive depth, resolve details, sense movement then track a moving object? Exactly how our eyes, which are receptors, and our brains, which filter and analyze the myriad data points our eyes perceive, manage to package the world we see for us is not wholly understood. For the purposes of this book, all you really need to know is that eyes react to light. The keys to this function of the eye are two sets of photoreceptor cells located in the retina called rods and cones. Rods, of which there are approximately 120 million per eye, gather information relating to light and movement and are also key elements in peripheral vision—our ability to perceive objects to the sides of our directed point of focus (i.e., "out of the corner of our eye").

Cones, which number only about 6 to 7 million and are centrally located in the retina, are both the eye's color receivers and the core of our visual acuity, our ability to perceive fine detail. They are less

The eyes' cone cells, specialized to perceive color, aren't much use when it comes to finding reed-colored owls in reed beds. But once this Short-eared Owl turns its head, 120 million motion-detecting rod cells come online.

sensitive to light than are rod cells, which is why our ability to perceive color is diminished in the dark.

Why do you need to know all this to find birds? You don't. But it is interesting and does support the point I made earlier. Your eyes, Mr. and Ms. Birding Machine, are jam-packed with cells designed to detect objects: rods! The cells we use to shop for clothes, read the installation instructions for a new software package, or text message our BBFs about what happened (OMG) last night are a distant numeric second.

Don't get me wrong, color is, at times, very helpful when it comes to locating birds. But basically it's the rod cells that are on the front line of bird finding. Cone cells get into the game when it's time to identify (and savor) birds.

Eye See, Therefore I Bird

As we all know, eyesight varies among individuals. Some people have remarkable eyesight—they are able to perceive color and detail way beyond the limits of the average person. I know a hawk watcher named Pete Both who was so good at picking out high-flying birds that among my hawk-watching confederates, birds flying at altitudes that were barely suborbital known as "Pete Both birds."

Translation: Forget looking for this one yourself. Only Pete Both could find it.

Other people are visually challenged, needing mechanical or surgical support to see what other people see normally, and some people face even greater visual challenges—including the challenge of not being able to see at all.

To those sight-challenged individuals I have two things to say. First, birds have you covered. Not only are birds a feast for the eyes, they are a feast for the ears. Second, you don't need to be a visual Einstein to be an accomplished bird finder.

Years ago, the Cape May Bird Observatory conducted an experiment to measure "counter bias" among different hawk counters. Five accomplished birders were involved in the program. Prior to the experiment, everyone's eyes were examined. Surprisingly, the range of visual acuity varied markedly. Some team members had very good eyesight—twenty-twenty or better. Some, despite their avocational focus, did not.

But this was not the greatest surprise. In addition to visual acuity, everyone's peripheral vision was tested, too—i.e., the capacity to perceive objects and motion outside the focus of directed vision, a region covered mostly by rod cells. For the average person, this lateral expanse covers less than 90 degrees.

The ophthalmologist administering the test set a device atop the head of the first counter—a contraption that looked like a cross between a Brownie Scout beanie and a wilting rabbit-ear TV antenna. At the end of each drooping antenna was a colored ball, which the ophthalmologist positioned on either side of the subject's head, about a foot from either ear.

"I'm going to move the balls slowly forward," the doctor directed. "Tell me when you can see them."

"I can see them," the counter said.

"No," the doctor explained again, "*wait* until I start to move the balls forward, then tell me when they come into view."

"I see them now," the counter repeated.

And so he did. So did the other four counters (plus me). Every one of us had peripheral vision that was about off the chart—180 degrees (or better). And while it is possible that all of us were simply born with superlative peripheral vision, I have a different explanation.

I believe that through years of birding, of searching for and finding birds that were often first detected out of "the corners of our eyes," we had simply expanded and strengthened our peripheral vision.

You sit in front of a computer all day playing World of Warcraft, your peripheral vision does about nothing. You spend your days trying not to be eaten by lions or finding birds out of the corners of your eyes, your peripheral vision gets a pretty good workout.

Birds Speak to Us

It's called bird watching, but experienced birders rely heavily upon their ears to detect and identify birds. During the World Series of Birding, a twenty-four-hour competition held every May in New Jersey, more than half the birds located by teams are grabbed by the ears—located and identified by the bird's song or call. Between midnight and dawn, virtually all birds tallied are found by sound (and accomplished teams commonly have more than thirty species tallied before it is light enough for the eye to detect movement or shape, much less color).

Often the first clue that a bird is nearby is auditory. The booming call of the Lesser Prairie-Chicken will lead you to the bird, and to the lek where courting males strut their stuff.

Birds call at night?

Absolutely. In fact, some birds, such as owls, rails, and nightjars, are most active and vocal at night. And many scores of bird species migrate at night, vocalizing as they travel.

But you don't need to be able to pin a name to a call for bird vocalizations to be useful. Often the first clue a birder has that a bird is nearby is auditory. Birds sing and call. They make noise when they forage. The wings on many species whistle or twitter as the birds fly. Birds landing or taking off may brush their wings against leaves or branches or open water.

Birds not only signal their own presence by vocalizing, they sometimes even signal the presence of other birds. A behavior called "mobbing" is common in many bird species, particularly woodland species. If a predatory animal is found (most commonly a bird-eating snake or owl) smaller birds gather around and hurl verbal abuse at the intruder. This harangue can be heard at great distances, and experienced birders know to investigate it.

Our ability to capture and analyze sound is as complex and fascinating as our ability to perceive the world visually. The organs that allow this auditory interface are our ears. What these do are

Roosting Northern Saw-whet Owls can be very hard to find. So let the professionals do it for you. When chickadees start scolding, savvy birders know to investigate.

gather and direct sound waves into a chamber that not only analyzes and organizes the components of sound but converts the waves into electrical impulses that are transmitted to our brain for further analysis.

Sound waves vary in frequency, and this frequency is measured in hertz (Hz), or cycles per second. The human ear is capable of capturing sounds that range from a low of 20 Hz to 20,000 Hz (which is a pretty fair chunk of the world's auditory array), although some marine mammals can hear sounds as low as 0.25 Hz, and bats can detect sounds as high as 120,000 Hz (way above the range of humans).

Key to this discussion is the realization that ears (and vocal mechanisms) of birds and humans operate at pretty much the same frequency range and that most bird sounds fall between 2,000 and 4,000 Hz.

In essence, birds speak to us (i.e., not above or below the normal range of human hearing). All we have to do is be attuned to their vocalizations.

So why aren't we?

Everything You Knew About Bird Finding You Learned, then Unlearned, in the Crib

Every child, at birth, is a John James Audubon waiting to happen—but it takes time. For the first few months of our lives, our eyes, ears, and, especially, brains are going through a rapid catch-up with the strange, new, stimulus-filled world we've been dumped into.

At birth, we perceive the world in undifferentiated shades of gray. A week after birth, we begin to perceive color. At two months, our eyes are able to adjust their focus. At three months, we can track and follow slow-moving objects. At five months, we're able to differentiate between our mother's face and that of a stranger.

Separating *Empidonax* flycatchers takes a little longer.

Hearing development is more protracted. At four months, babies react to sound. At seven months, they turn their heads in the direction of a voice speaking. At nine months, they turn around at a sound behind them.

The brain is working hard, too. Taking it all in. Working the world into some kind of cognitive framework.

Color, sound, mom, carrot puree, face of dog, wet, "ah goo goo, goo goo," crib, curtains, "tick-tock," window, tree, birdy . . .

Pretty birdy.

The world is one big sensory menu page and we are just sucking it all in, using our senses to gather data and our brain to sort, stack, and put it all into some kind of meaningful package.

This is where the problem begins—at our rapidly developing and overworked mental triage center. *Everything* is a great deal to assimilate, so pretty soon our brain begins assigning priority to stimulus. New things get high priority. Old things that seem not to have a great deal of bearing on our lives, such as the sound of a furnace going or the ticking of a grandfather clock, get short shrift.

It's not that our ears stop picking up the sounds of the furnace or the clock. It's just that our brain has stopped according them significance. It develops a sort of software package that filters these incoming impulses. Labels them "spam." Relegates them to the trash bin of our minds, where they won't overload our ability to function.

This gives our brains the latitude to deal with matters of consequence: mashed beets, alphabet blocks, the morning cartoon lineup, two-wheel bicycles, karate lessons, "four score and seven years ago," hanging out at the mall, line drives to left field, parallel parking, passing finals, studs

For the most part, the Audubon that "oughta been" disappeared in the crib—this young resident of Canada's Nunavut Territory excepted.

or hoops?, lunch with the boss, "till death do us part," "ah goo goo, goo goo" . . .

For most well-adjusted adults growing up in the twenty-first century, bird movement and bird sounds simply do not make it through our spam filter and into the inbox of our lives and daily routine.

With apologies to Ogden Nash: the Audubon you "oughta been" died in the crib.

You've got a lot of catching up to do. But at the very least, you have all the equipment you need: eyes and ears spec'ed for bird detection. You can go right outside and start using them.

2 | Where the Birds Are (and You Should Be)

There are thousands of bird species. There are billions of birds. But just like justice and cell phone service, birds are not evenly apportioned across the planet. They are rare in some places or environments, abundant and concentrated in others.

Want to practice good bird-finding skills the easy way? Go someplace where your efforts are going to give you a gratifying return. If you are willing to keep your expectations low, you won't necessarily have to go far.

One of my sub-hobbies is going to large metropolitan areas and seeing how many different species of birds I can find. Places like New York City, Chicago, Reno, and Minneapolis-St. Paul.

Different birds are suited for different habitats, and while relatively few birds are specifically designed to thrive in places dominated by brick, mortar, macadam, and neon, birds can be amazingly pliant, as my story about the Fort Lee TV crew illustrates.

My urban bird-finding expeditions always begin at dawn. They run for one hour. My route, rarely predetermined, is guided by two basic principles. I head downhill, and I head for trees whenever I see them. The more trees the better.

Why downhill? Because most cities are situated near oceans, lakes, or major rivers. Basic rule of thumb: You want birds, just add water. Water runs (and collects) downhill.

Why trees? Because most of the birds found in North America belong to a large scientific order known as the Passeriformes.

Passeriformes means "perching birds," i.e., birds whose feet are specialized for grasping perches.

As you might suspect, the perches nine out of ten perching birds give two alulas up to are perches associated with a tree (although utility lines are pretty popular, and there was a time when TV aerials were the rage among Northern Mockingbirds).

Our species has a penchant for trees, too. Most urban areas cater to this human predilection by creating parks and greenways. In fact, some urban oases are celebrated bird-watching sites.

Central Park in New York City is one of the planet's finest migratory hot spots. In spring and fall, migrating birds that find themselves over Manhattan around dawn look down. Size up what is, to their eyes, a sterile wasteland. Home in on this uptown patch of green sandwiched between Fifth and Eighth Avenues, seeing it as a verdant canyon bracketed by rocky cliffs.

But my downtown walks rarely intersect parks as large as Central Park. In fact, commonly, the most vegetated habitat I encounter is a tree-lined street.

How many birds can I expect to find on a one-hour sojourn in a large city? My average is fifteen species in summer or winter, slightly more in spring and fall. Is this how many species you might expect to see?

Uh . . . no. At least not until you finish reading this book and get a couple years of practice under your belt. Untutored, chances are

Perching birds such as this Greater Pewee constitute a large part of the avain lineup, and through the ages, perches associated with trees have consistently scored high among perching birds.

you'll see considerably fewer than fifteen species. In fact, you'll likely see less than half that number (and I'm including in your tally Rock Pigeon, House Sparrow, European Starling, and House Finch—the metropolitan big four).

Maybe in the lifestyle advocated and summarized by Woody Allen, a person can get away with "just showing up." But finding birds requires a measure of know-how and skill.

Timing Is Everything

Did you happen to clue in on that one piece of priceless information regarding the timing of my urban birding forays? Right. Dawn. It's one of the peak activity periods for most birds. The time they wake up. Get vocal. Get mobile—and much of this mobility involves foraging. For many species, for much of the year, foraging entails a daily commute between roosting and feeding areas.

Even in downtown urban areas, overhead airspace at dawn is crowded with incoming and outgoing bird traffic.

In summer, herons, swifts, and swallows rank among the most common morning commuters overflying urban areas. In winter, ducks, geese, and gulls are regular travelers.

Gulls? Part of the avifauna of inland cities? Absolutely. Gulls of multiple species, too. Most gulls are not dependent upon oceans—as scavengers, they are dependent upon a source of food. For many gulls, we are that source. Humans are a messy, profligate species. A nearby river or frozen reservoir to roost on, coupled with a garbage dump or fast-food parking lot, is all a gull needs to feel welcome. Thanks to us, locations that offer these two basic gull-supporting requirements are widespread.

So that's all there is to it? The way to find birds is simply to look up? It's one way. But not by any means the only way, or necessarily the best way, or even, for that matter, my immediate point here. The point I'm making is that birds have daily activity patterns. Synchronize your schedule with theirs and you'll find more birds.

From dawn until mid-morning (about ten o'clock) is the peak activity period for most birds. It's when territorial males are most vocal. It's also when birds are feeding heavily.

Dawn. It's one of the peak activity periods for birds and birders. These birders perched on the Higbee Beach dike in Cape May are searching the morning skies for migrating warblers.

From late afternoon until dusk, when birds are returning to roost sites or feeding up for the night, is another peak activity period (although vocalizations among most species are not as spirited then). In general, midday hours are the nadir of bird activity.

But not for all species. Soaring birds, such as hawks, eagles, pelicans, and cranes, are often most evident just when other birds begin to call it a morning. Soaring birds are mostly dependent upon thermals to gain altitude, and thermals are generated by the sun's heating rays. Between nine-thirty and ten o'clock in the morning, the angle of the sun is right for thermals to form. Soaring birds seek out these heated columns of air and ride them aloft, where they are, at least for a time, easily viewed.

They do this when they migrate. They do this to relocate within what are, for many species, large territories.

They also do it just to be seen!

No, not by you. As already mentioned, birds are not vain. The reason many birds go aloft is to post notice of occupancy to neighbors (or would-be neighbors) or engage in a little dyad maintenance with their mate.

The activity pattern of some other species is tied more closely to the tide cycle than the clock. Many shorebirds (such as sandpipers and plovers) flock to mudflats exposed by low tide, and many gulls and sea ducks also time their feeding accordingly (so they won't have to dive so far for shellfish). When the tide comes in, the birds

Soaring birds are often most evident after others have called it a morning. These northbound Anhingas migrating over the Rio Grande are one of many species that use thermals for lift.

quit the flats—but they don't disappear. They relocate to roosting areas on higher ground where they wait for the next tide.

There are other factors and conditions that cause birds to relocate and concentrate—some periodic and opportune. These will be treated in a separate chapter.

But there are several very salient factors that have a great deal to do with finding birds: distribution, or the geographic range that a species occupies, and seasonality, or the geographic redistribution of many species. But perhaps the *most* salient factor is habitat. Different birds are suited to exploit the advantages of different habitats. Go to the right habitat and you'll find them there again, and again, and again.

Book Smart and Habitat Stupid

When I was seven, my bird field guide was a pocket-sized book with American Robins on the cover and the depictions and descriptions of 112 birds "in full color" within. It was a great book, a catalytic book, and if anyone asks me why I'm a bird-watcher today, I'll direct them to that Golden Nature Guide.

Over the course of several years, I managed to find most of the 112 birds depicted in the book in the woods behind my parents' home.

Including Blue Jay (which was my favorite).

And Wood Thrush (which replaced Blue Jay as my favorite).

And "Rufous-sided" Towhee (which bumped Wood Thrush).

And Rose-breasted Grosbeak (which was my absolute, all-time favorite . . . until I saw my first Wood Duck, and then that became . . .).

Just one thing puzzled me. In fact, it frustrated me. As expert a birder as (I thought) I was and as hard as I tried, I just couldn't find some of the birds that were depicted in the book.

Even though the range maps said they were right *here!*

"Here," by the way, was Whippany, New Jersey, the birding epicenter of the universe in the 1950s. My universe, anyway.

I mean, OK, I could see how a kid growing up in Whippany, New Jersey, was never going to see a Magpie. According to the range map drawn for each species, Magpies were found only in the West. But what about Horned Lark?! A real cool-looking bird (that even had horns), and the range map said it was *right where I lived—* in fact, it said it was where I lived *in purple!*

Purple was the color that said birds were found in a place all year (like House Sparrows . . . and I sure had no trouble finding House Sparrows).

All year! But hard as I tried, I still couldn't find one measly Horned Lark. Or Vesper Sparrow (a bird that looked a lot like Song Sparrow but had white outer tailfeathers and a much cooler name than Song Sparrow). Ditto Bobolink, which the book said was "easy to identify." Or meadowlark, which was another of those birds with an all-purple rating.

Maybe you've already diagnosed the problem. About the time I reached age ten and augmented my birding library with books that were more generous in their scope of information, I did too. The idea of range I understood. Seasonality, too. What I'd failed to appreciate was habitat and how closely linked birds are to the habitat they are specialized to use.

My childhood birding haunts were woodlands. The birds I was having such a hard time finding were all grassland species. More than fifty years on, I've seen thousands of Horned Larks and Bobolinks and a pretty fair number of meadowlarks (of two species) and Vesper Sparrows, too.

The Horned Lark is a real cool bird that I aspired to see when I first started birding. But to my consternation, I could never locate this common and widespread grassland species in the woodlands behind my home.

But to this day, I've never seen any of these grassland species in woodlands, and chances are I never will.

One of the last things birders gain an appreciation for is also one of the most basic and determining. Bird are almost always found where they are supposed to be.

They are creatures of habit and habitat. There is rhyme and reason, a cause-and-effect relationship between *what* a bird is and *where* it is, and some of these links can be very specific.

Solitary Sandpiper is a freshwater obligate. Unlike Greater and Lesser Yellowlegs, it does not forage in tidal wetlands. Seaside Sparrow, on the other hand, is found *only* in tidal wetlands. If you want to see one, simply traveling to the Atlantic or Gulf coast is insufficient. You also need to go to a salt marsh.

Montezuma Quail are relegated to pine-oak woodlands on arid slopes with a grassy substrate. Kirtland's Warbler breed only in young Jack Pine forest found almost exclusively in northern Michigan.

And Horned Lark? The bird I aspired to see in my youth? Open, treeless, often denuded substrate with scant grass and lots of bare earth is its preferred habitat. *Anything* but forest.

If you are looking for a specific bird, start with the habitat that supports it. Chances are your search will end there, too. Successfully.

But before you start searching, there are some things you need to know.

Garbing Yourself for Close Encounters of an Avian Kind

Every avocation has an idiosyncratic dress code—a type or style of clothing that is tied to function and need (although why some golfers are drawn to wear pants so garish they wouldn't be accepted at a thrift store is beyond me).

Bicyclists wear clothing that is light, pliant, and tight fitting (to reduce drag). Quail hunters wear clothing that is brier-proof and bright orange to promote situational awareness. Gardeners wear wide-brimmed floppy hats, button-down long-sleeve shirts, and jeans. And birders . . .

Birders wear just about anything they want to wear, and this latitude is tied mostly to weather and climate, because birding is something that is conducted in just about every environment imaginable—desert, tropical rainforest, arctic seas, arid grasslands, tidal flats, alpine tundra, city parks . . .

If you are birding California's Salton Sea in August, you will be wearing shorts (probably grimy), a bird festival T-shirt, and a wraparound, air-conditioned airport rental car. If you are birding the Pribilofs in June, you are wearing Gortex everything (underneath your Helly Hansens) and knee-length rubber boots. If you are birding Newburyport, Massachusetts, in January, you are wearing every piece of warm clothing you own (and it still won't be enough).

There are only a couple of considerations that birders should bear in mind when choosing field clothing. First, garments must be quiet—rustle and swish free. It's not so much that you don't want birds to hear you. But you do want to hear birds. Clothing that makes you sound like you've been gift wrapped for the holidays isn't going to help your cause.

There's another important consideration that birders should bear in mind: Birds see colors, and bright colors are more conspicuous than muted ones. If your objective is to get close to birds, you are probably better off wearing neutral or natural colors rather than colors suitable for the Mardi Gras parade.

Experts are divided on this subject—to what degree birds are sensitive to or troubled by bright colors. All I can tell you is that no bird photographer goes into the field wearing hot pink or blaze

Visually and audibly quiet clothing is the fashion in birding. Granted, my rain gear here adds an element of swish, swish to biped locomotion—but it's better than being cold and wet in the Canadian Arctic.

orange. Most wear hunting camo, as I do when I'm deer hunting and very often when birding, too.

Sitting in a tree stand in full camo, I am habitually engaged by birds that fly close, trying to make out what manner of creature is sitting in the tree. On multiple occasions, I've had chickadees land on the barrel of my gun (or my hat). I've had Brown Creepers and White-breasted Nuthatches (and flying squirrels) climb my pants leg.

Me? I think bright colors in the field are not a good idea, and wearing cryptic colors like brown, tan, and dark green gives birders an edge when it comes to getting close to birds.

One thing I absolutely believe is that white is to be avoided. Across the animal world, white is the signal for danger. A deer, sensing danger, raises a white flag (its tail). A school of fish, being attacked by a predator, gather in a tight group and turn as one, flashing white undersides.

We're not talking just jackets, shirts, and pants here. The birding ban on white extends to footgear, too. Consider: You are walking down a trail at a prime birding hot spot. You turn the corner. Bring your evolutionarily honed eyes to bear and see . . .

Nothing. Odd, you think.

No, nothing odd about it. You should have been here a split second ago—the second before your bright white sneakers flashed into view. Birds have very quick reaction times, and their M.O. when alerted to potential danger is to bolt first and ask questions later.

If you want to see more birds, don't wear white. And absolutely, absolutely don't wear white if you want to go birding with me.

What About Binoculars?

Well, what about them? You need them to watch birds. Plain and simple. But the subject of this book is finding birds, and for the most part birds are located with the unaided human eye.

This is not an inviolate rule. In fact, as a person who has spent thousands of hours scanning the skies for hawks and oceans for seabirds, I can assure you that there are situations and species groups for which scanning with binoculars (or a spotting scope) is the default setting.

But think a minute. Think of the advantages that are diminished or nullified when you bring binoculars up to your eyes. Right off the bat, your view of the world is reduced by about ninety-five percent. Good binoculars offer a field of view that is about 8 degrees of arc. Your eyes, with birder-enhanced peripheral vision, give you between 100 and 180 degrees of arc. You bring binoculars to your eyes, you've just thrown away your greatest bird-finding advantage—your ability to perceive the whole world in front of you. You gave this away for a magnified slice.

Sure, you need binoculars for birding. But for the most part, when birding, it's the eyes that find and the binoculars that study.

Also, you need to focus binoculars manually—something your eyes do automatically. And when you look through binoculars, you are bringing not only your eyes but your mind to bear—telling your brain that what it should be concentrating on is the image framed by the circle. So directed, subtle clues—like a bird calling softly, like a rustle in the leaves—may go unnoticed.

More often than not, finding birds means *expanding* your awareness, not focusing it. And while you might be immensely proud of your new binoculars and love the supernatural intimacy they bring, don't lose sight of your objective here.

The eye finds. The binoculars study. That's how the game is mostly played.

Playing the Field . . . and the Trees

OK. You've got the innate skills. You've got quiet clothing (with quiet colors). You've got a morning free. Let's go birding.

The question is, where? And while I can answer this in the broadest sense (someplace nearby where you'll find birds), the specific location is up to you. I don't know where you live.

What you are looking for is some fairly sizable natural area big enough to support year-round resident species (like woodpeckers, chickadees, and jays) and seasonal residents, too: birds that arrive in the spring to breed, or birds that relocate there in the fall to spend the winter.

Ideally, you'll want someplace that offers a mix of habitat. Mature forest. Healthy understory. Open fields. Marshy areas or swamps. An adjacent lake, river, or pond. Remember, different species use different habitats. Want to boost the number of birds you see? Boost the variety of habitats you visit.

You're going to want a good, smooth trail system (because your eyes are going to be too busy to mind your feet). You're going to want someplace where you feel safe. This may mean a place where other people go to enjoy some time outdoors.

A local park. A bike or walking or jogging trail. Not only do such places offer security (in numbers), they feature birds that are habituated to people—birds that are easy to see and easy to approach because they've come to understand that people pose no threat.

Need someplace to go birding? This spot looks good: Elements include open, obstruction-free trails, flanking woodlands, and fields beyond. It's a stretch of the planet I navigated almost every day in my youth, so I can vouch for its birding potential.

Other prime birding locations include municipal, county, state, and national parks; monuments; and national recreation areas. The U.S. Fish and Wildlife Service maintains more than 550 National Wildlife Refuges, a quarter of which are found in or adjacent to urban centers. In addition, individual states maintain areas for sports fishing and hunting that are open to birders.

Note: If you are birding land set aside for hunting during hunting season, my advice governing the use of cryptic clothing should be amended by including in your wardrobe a blaze-orange cap or vest. Do this for your own personal safety. Do it also as a courtesy to hunters who will be expecting other people in the field to know and follow proper protocol. Don't own any blaze-orange outerwear? Stay out of the woodlands open to hunters during hunting season.

There are national forests, national grasslands, and millions of acres of open space maintained by the Bureau of Land Management. In addition, there are private, not-for-profit organizations like the Nature Conservancy and the Audubon Society that own natural areas that are open to the public (often for a fee).

If you go online, you can type in "bird watching locations in (fill in your state, county, or municipality)." Or, if you want to gain an experienced birder's edge right out of the blocks, type in "bird watching organizations in (your state)" and see what comes up. Sign up or show up for a regularly scheduled bird walk or field trip. Learn where the hot local birding locations are.

But that's for next time. You're ready to go birding right now. So let's do it. But let's also do it right.

3 | The Elements of Bird Finding

The Beverly Hillbillies was a sitcom sensation back in the 1960s, and its enduring popularity as a TV rerun attests to this. But wittingly or unwittingly, the producers of the show set bird watching back a generation by adding to the cast an austere looking, overly cerebral, straitlaced bank president's secretary whose hobby was, you guessed it, bird watching. At odd intervals, Jane Hathaway would be shown slinking through the woodlands like a ninja with an inner ear problem, head raised and binoculars fused to her eyes. Her look of concentration could melt lead. Her movements and manner (and demeanor) could not have been more stereotypically wrong.

First, nobody peers through binoculars while walking. It's no way to find birds, and it's a great way to twist an ankle, break a wrist, or worse, wreck your binoculars when you use them to try and break your fall.

Second, there's no need or reason to crouch or slink or pirouette in slow mo. The birds know you're there. If anything, you are going to make them suspicious by acting so weird.

The proper and most effective M.O. is to simply walk slowly along with binoculars hanging from your neck (or, if you anticipate birds, in your hands). Slowly turn your head to study the habitat around you. Use your eyes to detect motion and your ears to pick up, then pinpoint, sounds.

If you see movement or hear birds, STOP either immediately or at the nearest point that gives you the proximity, stable footing, angle, or view you want. Sometimes this means moving very slowly forward. Sometimes it means taking a step or two back.

A word on etiquette: If you are on a busy trail (such as a bike path), you and others will be well served if you move to the side before anchoring yourself on the path and raising binoculars to your eyes. Binoculars up, you've just brought your whole focus to bear, and things like people rollerblading may stop being a concern to you—but they remain a hazard.

The Power of Pause

Now wait. You've stopped moving. You own this moment.

Your own movement—the rolling image of the world going by—is no longer masking your detection mechanisms. Millions of years of evolutionary refinement are on your side, and you are bringing them to bear.

That's right, Mr. and Ms. Twenty-first-century American. You are hunting. You are gathering.

Very possibly, the bird you detected has paused, too. You've just broken the pattern. Stopped when everyone else walks (or jogs or rollerblades) by. It's waiting and watching, too.

But birds are animate creatures by nature. They move. And since you've chosen to bird at a time when birds are actively feeding, chances are this bird is searching for food. Sooner or later— about as soon as it takes for the bird to conclude that you pose no immediate threat—it will resume doing whatever it was doing that caught your eye or ear.

Never underestimate the power of pause. When you stop moving, your eyes become more sensitive to motion, and birds may betray their presence. This female Dusky Grouse caught my eye when she tried to slink away undetected.

Actually, and as a matter of course, it is a good idea to pause now and again whether you see or hear a bird or not. The sound of your footsteps muffles bird noises. A world in motion confuses your eyes. Stop wherever you find a place that offers a good, open view or a spot that has a bountiful crop of berries or an area where you have found birds before.

Pausing also prompts some birds to move or fly—birds that you would have walked right by. Your sudden immobility suggests to a perched Cooper's Hawk that it's been seen. Or because you stopped, the Ruffed Grouse crouched in the wild grape tangle just off the trail that had been monitoring your approach has now lost track of you. Using the principle better safe than sorry, the bird rockets off in a blur of wings or, if you are lucky, elects to slink away—Jane Hathaway style. Just with more style.

Three Key Points

1. When you stop, space your feet for anchorage and balance. You are about to bring binoculars up to your eyes. It's going to scramble your sense of balance. A quick, corrective step to keep yourself from falling is going to set the bird appearance clock back to zero (and it might flush any bird that is studying you). Also, try and pick a place that is not in the middle of last year's crunchy leaves or, if you are on pavement, roadside gravel. Hearing birds goes better with silence, and I am constantly astonished by people who continue to shuffle their feet in a noisy substrate when a quiet alternative lies a step away.

2. If you find yourself staring into the sun in a direction where there is glare, try and find a shadow to stand in—something that will block the glare. This will make it easier not only to spot the bird but to see the color and detail you want. With your eyes shaded, your pupils expand, admitting more light and allowing your eyes to perceive more color and detail. (Didn't you ever wonder why Native American braves were always putting their open hands to their foreheads to shield their eyes?)

3. You should try and gauge the approximate distance to the bird. If you are in a woodland, it is likely a matter of feet, not football-field lengths. Grasp your binoculars and slowly raise them to your chin, *but do not bring them to your eyes and start searching for the bird.*

Remember, eyes find; binoculars study.

One thing you might do, while you are waiting for the bird to show, is to prefocus your instrument down to the approximate distance to your expected target. Binoculars have a range of focus—from infinity to about eight feet or less (for good birding binoculars). When you bring your binoculars up to your eyes, it helps to have them ballpark-close to the proper point of focus (otherwise, all you'll see when you look through them is a blur, and you'll waste precious seconds spinning your focus wheel).

If the bird is, say, approximately thirty feet away and your binoculars focus down to eight feet, try turning the wheel all the way to the closest point of focus then spinning it back a quarter turn. This will put you in the ballpark. Now when you get on the bird, focusing will be a matter of small adjustment, not full revolutions of the wheel.

I SEE IT!

Good for you. Now, keeping your eye on the bird, raise your binoculars until they fall in line with you and the bird. Focus. And keep your finger on the focus wheel. The bird is probably going to move. You'll follow it in the glass, or you'll need to relocate the bird with your unaided eyes and bring your binoculars to bear again. Either way, you'll probably need to readjust the focus.

If you don't see the bird when you bring binoculars to your eyes, wait. The bird may simply be motionless. Give it a chance to move and your eyes a chance to distinguish it.

If it becomes obvious that your binoculars are not trained on the bird, *do not search back and forth, up and down, for the bird with your binoculars.* Lower the bins (so you are looking over them). Relocate the bird with your eyes. Keeping your eyes on the bird, raise the binoculars and try again.

Got it? Good. Now comes the challenging part. Now you have to identify the bird. And now you're on your own. Sorry. Bird identification is not the focus of this book.

Next, Please

The fascinating thing, maybe the best thing, about birding is that while the bird you are studying is gratifying, the bird you are not seeing (yet) is alluring. If birding is likened to a treasure hunt, the treasure still on the beach shines brighter than that gathered in your coffer. After a satisfying (or frustrating) encounter with a bird, you'll want to move on. You'll want to find more birds.

But take a good look around before leaving the bird you just found, because birds tend to be social. Where there is one, there are often more (and often several or even many more). Woodland birds tend to be flocking birds (except during the breeding season). There is safety in numbers. What is attractive to one bird might be useful to another.

And, as mentioned, birds are not uniformly spaced or apportioned across the planet. As you search, you'll likely navigate birdless stretches and then, suddenly, you're into birds.

Suddenly, but not necessarily unpredictably (and certainly not without cause). Birds have certain basic requirements. They concentrate where their needs are met.

If you understand what motivates birds, you'll find more of them, more often.

Oh, the Birds You'll See

A typical good birding area offers a mix of habitat. Some habitats will be manifestly different—like a riparian woodland corridor snaking through prairie, the corridor dominated by mature cottonwoods, the prairie by grasses and flowers. Some differ in degrees— like a forest glen undergoing the early stages of succession (hence a patch of sapling trees surrounded by older, more mature trees). Believe it or not, there are different species specialized to live in these two different woodland habitats.

Different birds are specialized for different habitats: Clapper Rails (top left) spend much of their time skulking through tidal wetlands. Greater Shearwaters (top right) spend their lives at sea. Hermit Thrushes (right) are common birds of the forest floor and understory.

HERMIT THRUSH PHOTO
BY MICHAEL HANNISIAN

There are birds specialized to live in the tall canopy. Birds that thrive in dense understory. Bird specialized to forage (even nest) on the forest floor.

There are birds, such as rosy finches, that eke out a living in alpine tundra—where ice, rock, and vegetation meet. Birds such as Clapper Rails, which spend much of their lives tucked in a marsh-grass fortress. Birds such as Greater Shearwaters, which spend their lives in marine environments (coming to land only to nest).

There is no single place to see all the birds a continent (much less a planet!) has to offer. But the basics remain the same. Birds need food. They need shelter to roost and avoid life-sapping conditions. At times, they need to secure a mate and breed. At certain times, of the day and the year, they need to relocate.

But let's finish our walk. And learn a bit about the cause-and-effect relationship between birds, habits, and habitat along the way.

Moving On

So the bird you saw was, let's say, a Hermit Thrush—a common bird of the forest that is widespread across North America (and a favorite of mine). It is the only spot-breasted thrush that winters north of Mexico. Its song is dreamy, ethereal, shifting.

But now you hear high-pitched birdcalls coming from somewhere ahead. Not at eye-level or below (like the thrush) but higher up, in the canopy. It sounds like more than one bird (something you'll discover is pretty typical in "feeding flocks"), and with your eyes searching for the source of the sound, it's not too long before you spot movement and the forms of several small birds moving through the canopy.

If you don't already know the call notes of chickadees, you should. They and their confederates the titmice form the core of feeding flocks across much of North America. (In scrub, open woodlands, and commonly drier portions of the West, a close relative, the Bushtit, serves as a bellwether bird.)

For the most part, chickadees and titmice are year-round residents. They and birds such as nuthatches, woodpeckers, kinglets, and Brown Creepers team up and move through woodlands searching for food.

During migration, small woodland migrants commonly join these feeding flocks. And while these transient birds may be silent, the vocal locals are not.

Train your ears to be alert for chickadee vocalizations and the calls of other perennial (or seasonal) members of the local flock. Change your course to intercept them. First find the birds. Notice the direction the flock is moving. Maneuver to get ahead of it.

While chickadees of several species are permanent residents, feeding flocks are not permanent fixtures in woodlands. They coalesce in late summer and disband in spring. They do this because during the breeding season the members of the flock pair off, establish territories, get on with the very important matter of courtship, breeding, and rearing young.

However, and just as useful from the standpoint of locating birds, during the breeding season, territorial male birds are very vocal. Many birds, particularly woodland songbirds, sing rings around their territories with song—a vocal performance that is commonly more rich and varied than the simple utterances or "call notes" birds use throughout the year.

In spring and early summer, finding birds is hardly more difficult than detecting their songs and following your ears to the source. Territorial birds begin singing at dawn. Early in the season, before mates are secured, males may sing off and on all day. Later in the season, the "dawn chorus" may last for only an hour. By July, over most of North America, woodlands (and grasslands and marshes) have grown seasonally silent. With the breeding season over, there is little reason for song.

Except during the breeding season, when hungry young are in the nest, by midmorning most bird activity has tapered off dramatically. Territorial birds are no longer singing. Foraging flocks have stopped foraging. It's time to get out of the woods and into the open, where other birds (and challenges) await.

Courtship and pair bonding occur early for many raptors, even during the winter months in some locations. These adult Bald Eagles appear to be past the initial courtship stage.

4 | New Challenges, New Opportunities, New Horizons, New Shores

Over the course of my life, I've been treated to unassailable truisms that weren't. Things like: "Property is always your best investment."

Well, here is one truism you can take to the bank.

"If you want birds, just add water."

As much as food, as much as shelter, with few exceptions, birds need water. You find it, you find them.

Many species, such as ducks and geese, loons, grebes, herons, egrets, assorted shorebirds, and some highly specialized species like kingfishers and dippers, are dependent upon it. Some pelagic (ocean) species, such as petrels, shearwaters, and alcids, rarely leave it. Most land birds need water to drink and bathe. Some birds are bound to habitats that are at least semiaquatic. These include freshwater and saltwater marsh birds like rails and several species of blackbirds and sparrows.

If you are birding in arid grasslands or desert habitat and want to see birds, find a spring (or a campground spigot) and wait. As the day heats up, birds show up—quail, thrashers, sparrows . . . and don't be surprised if you find yourself sharing the watering hole. You aren't the only bird hunter in town. Foxes, coyotes, bobcats, and assorted birds of prey know all about birds and watering holes.

On the Pawnee Grasslands of Colorado, during dry years, I find it productive to stake out cattle tanks in midafternoon. There

If you want birds, just add water. On a hot day, treetop specialists such as the Western Tanager (top left) can be driven to the ground, grassland birds such as the Lark Bunting (top right) will join the herd, and American Goldfinches (left) will line up for sips at a fountain.

have been occasions when Horned Larks and Lark Buntings had to wait their turn to gain perch space on the rim of well-filled water tanks.

If you are conducting a Christmas Bird Count and your territory is snow covered, with all the lakes and rivers frozen, the iron rule of *agua* applies. Find water. Any open water. That's where the birds will be. Or bird.

One frigid CBC, I found a Lesser Yellowlegs, the day's *only* Lesser Yellowlegs, standing in a roadside seep of open brackish water the size of a pie plate. There were hundreds of acres of tidal wetlands in our area (all frozen) but only this single patch of open water was kept ice-free by sun-warmed asphalt.

Another time, in a Cape May blanketed by a foot of snow, I came across an American Woodcock foraging on the bare (and thawed) ground beneath a dripping outside faucet.

In Cape May, in migration, one of the things that seems true of migrating songbirds is that the morning after songbirds arrive, they occupy a variety of woodland habitat. But over the course of subsequent hours and days, these migrants gravitate toward, and concentrate in, wet woodlands and hardwood swamps, especially in dry years.

Our species has a penchant for water sources, too, and many of the trails found in natural areas are designed to intersect (if not follow or circumnavigate) wetlands. So, when woodlands begin to quiet down around midday, a good strategy for birders is to break from the trees and bring their attention to bear on marshes, streamsides, lakes, ponds, and beaches, and adjacent environments.

Out in the Open

One of the good things about birding open areas (marshes, beaches, grasslands, deserts, and tundra) is that there are not a lot of leaves and branches blocking your view. Birds are generally easier to see. The problem is, visibility cuts both ways. You are easier to see, too, and while your objective is to get close to birds, birds have just the opposite ambition. They want to maintain a comfortable distance from you, and, unfortunately, it is they, not you, that determine what this threshold is.

You'll know it when you get there. The bird will signal it by moving away.

Some birds swim. Some birds walk or run. Most birds fly, and this marvelous adaptation is one of the principal reasons bird watching is so challenging.

And frustrating.

Different species have different flush distances. Some, like bitterns, quail, and assorted grassland species, may allow birders to almost step on them before they explode into flight. Other birds, most notably many birds of prey, think a hundred, even two hundred, yards is plenty close enough.

There are things you can do to ensure that your sense of "close enough" falls short of their notion of "too close."

First, in the open, take your time. Your objective is to locate birds before you stumble upon and flush them. Be particularly mindful of the habitat ahead. Your sudden appearance near elevated perches (where birds might be posting sentry duty) or blind spots (like a bulrush-rimmed cove where birds are likely to seek shelter) is bound to make birds flush.

When scanning open areas with binoculars, what you are searching for are anomalies—like a fence post with a Common Nighthawk cap.

And yes, it's fine, even advisable, to also use binoculars to scan, to cut the distance and nullify the advantage birds have over us (superior eyesight). Bring your binoculars to your eyes and pan, slowly, turning from the waist, not your neck.

This isn't like looking for woodland birds. Small movements are harder to detect at a distance (and chances are, any bird you are close enough to see is busy watching you and so may be immobile or moving surreptitiously). What you are searching for are anomalies: an anomalous shape (a fence post with a nighthawk cap) or patch of color different enough to catch and hold your eye.

On a recent CBC, I picked out an Eastern Meadowlark by scanning an open field. At a quarter of a mile, if the bird's back had been toward me, it's certain I would have missed it. Head on, the minute spot of yellow against corn-stubble brown was just anomalous enough to warrant training a spotting scope on the possibility—one that this time turned into our only meadowlark of the day.

You say you don't have a spotting scope?

Then you'll just have to get closer, won't you?

OneTwoThreeFourFiveSixSevenEightNineTen RED LIGHT or the Ancient Art of Getting Close

There was a time, and it wasn't long ago, that just about every kid growing up in North America knew how to get close to animals.

Rabbits, snakes, turtles, frogs, deer, dads sleeping in hammocks, birds.

Especially birds (although in my time, I was a pretty fair hand at catching turtles and bullfrogs). I once even managed to stalk a sleeping rabbit and grab it with a one-hand snag. One of my favorite childhood pastimes was seeing how close I could get to feeding deer.

It's challenging, but not impossible. You approach from behind. Advance when the deer drops its head to feed. Stop when it raises its head and looks around.

It is a little like playing the game "red light," except deer are better at detecting motion than the person rattling off numbers is, and when you are caught moving, instead of you being the one sent back to the starting line, it is the deer that makes tracks.

With patience (and luck and a little cover) it's not hard to get within fifty feet of deer (and often you can get much closer than this with birds). Now back to birds.

First of all, note the wind direction. Birds take off into the wind. If you are approaching with the wind at your back (and in the bird's face) it will flush sooner than it would if its initial effort to avoid you didn't mean it would have to first fly toward you. If the wind direction is wrong—blowing from you toward the bird— circle around until you are approaching the bird downwind.

Here's another trick. Don't approach the bird directly—on a course plainly designed to intercept it. Plot an oblique course, one that will pass wide of the bird. This will keep the bird at ease (or at least keep it guessing about your intentions).

As you draw close, keep your eye on the bird. Watch for signs of nervousness (raised head, walking, or hopping). If the bird seems restless, stop and wait. Give it time to get used to you. This may take minutes. Try kneeling or sitting to present a less-threatening profile. When the bird calms down, advance obliquely. Often, before flying, birds turn into the wind and defecate. When this happens, chances are the bird has already elected to fly.

But it may fly only a short distance. To the next good perch. Now, at least, you know how far you can push it—but if you decide to approach again right away, you'll find that the bird will likely not let you get as close as the first time. Best to wait a while. Let the bird calm down. After five or ten minutes, the bird might be in a less suspicious frame of mind.

One last tip: As you approach, be mindful of other birds (or mammals) that you might stumble upon and flush. Waterfowl are particularly skittish and prone to suggestion. When one duck jumps, very commonly they all jump (and more often than not, they don't come back).

This is not always the case with some other species—including such very different birds as Wilson's Snipe and Sprague's Pipit.

Sprague's Pipit. A mouse in bird's clothing. This bug-eyed prairie specialty is easy to find when it's breeding. The male's towering display flight goes on for many minutes. But in winter, the birds melt into the grass. Flush when they are underfoot. Circle, land, and are swallowed by the earth once more.

When this happens, mark the spot. Don't take your eyes off it. Note anything that can be used as a marker. A darker patch of grass. A cow pie. Approach, slowly, to about forty or fifty feet. Scan the area with your binoculars. The bird is there, or at least in the vicinity. It may have scurried from the place it landed but it's still in the area. Chances are it is even looking at you. Only its grass-colored head is visible.

If you have a pure heart, you're sure to see it.

That's All There Is to It?

Yes. Basically. That and having a pure heart. But the operative word here is "basically" because most of what you've read so far has to deal with applying innate skills (your powers of detection) and fundamental principles (go slow, pause often, watch the birdy).

From here on in you will be polishing and refining your bird-finding skills, and this takes practice. Every trip afield, every bird seen, is a lesson that lays down reactive pathways in your mind. Birds are creatures of habit and habitat. What one does, one time, it or another member of its kind or tribe will likely do again. Your job is to assimilate this wisdom.

My father used to take a daily walk that led around the ponds in the woods behind our home. Every fall, about late September, he would announce that "the Great Blue Heron is back in his usual spot." He was almost right. Yes, every September, when Great Blue Herons migrate, the cove in the Third Brickyard Pond became a favorite fishing hole for this species. But every year it was a juvenile bird, a bird hatched that year and so a heron making the journey for the first time. Great Blue Herons are no more likely to pass on the location of favorite fishing holes than human fishermen are, but good fishermen, both human and avian, know a good spot when they see one.

So the first challenge new birders face is broadening their awareness. Sharpening their detection skills. Learning to react quickly and appropriately. In time, with experience, you'll develop and refine bird-finding skills. You'll be able to anticipate, even predict, the movements and appearance of birds. To nonbirders, this may seem like magic. And, as with magic, there is something hidden behind the magician's cape.

Years ago, I used to lead birding trips to Kenya for New Jersey Audubon. My favorite driver was a Kikuyu man named Matibo. Matibo had great eyes and knew the turf (driving the safari circuit with a new tour, as he did, every several weeks). But one day, Matibo pulled a rabbit out of a thorntree cap that astonished even me.

We were tooling along at about forty-five miles per hour when Matibo applied the brakes, started backing up. And in response to my unasked question said, "stone curlew."

Sure enough. A hundred feet back, and fifty yards off the road, a Spotted Stone Curlew was crouched, in the shadows, beneath the protective confines of a particularly ferocious-looking acacia. Even through binoculars, the cryptically colored bird (sitting as immobile as its name implies) was almost invisible.

"How did you ever see that?" I marveled.

Matibo, as was his wont, merely laughed.

It just so happened that on this trip, I was leading two tours back to back. Three weeks later, we were driving down the same road. Once again, Matibo applied the brakes. Backed up. And started offering the members of my group directions to the "stone curlew" resting in the shadow of the acacia (but not before passing a sheepish glance my way).

Creatures of habit. Go forth and learn them.

Rhyme and Reason and Seasonality, Too

Now that you have the idea that there is a cause-and-effect relationship between the location and movements of birds, here's a seasonal qualifier. The daily pattern of birds adjusts as their needs change, and these changes are mostly linked to season.

Let's go back to that trail where you saw the Hermit Thrush and the chickadees. The chickadees, as mentioned, are permanent residents—always found in the woodlands or riparian corridor or park you were birding. The Hermit Thrush is not. In summer, it breeds throughout the forests of Alaska and Canada and New England and in forests found at higher altitudes in the Rockies and Appalachians. In winter, it abandons almost all of its breeding range and relocates across the southern third of the U.S. and coastally north to extreme southern British Columbia and Massachusetts.

It turns out that most of the birds found in the Northern Hemisphere are migratory to some degree, and many other birds that can be found all year in a location change their habits in response to changing seasons.

Take, for example, the American Robin—perhaps the best-known bird species in North America. Most people hold to the belief that robins head south in the winter and return in the spring. Yes, they do. And if you live in a place where winters are characterized by prolonged cold and standing snow, you probably don't see robins until March or April.

But where I live, in southern New Jersey, we have robins in our yard from March through October. We also have thousands of robins flying over our house every morning November through February. Millions of American Robins winter in South Jersey. They roost in White Cedar stands and forage during the day on holly berries in coastal woodlands.

Millville, the region's shopping hub, is nicknamed the Holly City with reason.

So here, and in many parts of North America, robins don't necessarily "leave" in the winter. They relocate, change their pattern. In summer, they stake out suburban lawns within relatively small territories, feasting mostly on earthworms. In winter, when the ground is frozen (and earthworms retreat deeper into the soil) the birds switch over to a fruit diet and commute greater distances.

Winter (November through March/April)

The basic winter pattern of many bird species is to gather in mixed or single-species flocks and concentrate in places where they find shelter to roost and food to survive. This pattern and strategy are practiced by assorted waterbirds, game birds, shorebirds, seabirds, and gulls, and lots of songbirds, including larks, swallows, bluebirds, pipits, waxwings, many sparrow species, assorted blackbirds, and finches. Some species of raptor, like Northern Harriers and Short- and Long-eared Owls, roost communally but forage separately. Bald Eagles, on the other hand, may roost communally and concentrate during the day where food is available—at the base of open spillways or along open watercourses when everything else is frozen solid.

The trick to finding winter birds is finding where they are feeding or where they are roosting or resting and heading there, or putting yourself on the commuter route between these two poles of the winter pattern. The birds are massed and concentrated, facilitating detection. They are bound by their needs, giving you a strategic advantage.

Also in late winter and early spring, some bird species may already be engaged in active courtship. Northern Harriers; Cooper's,

In winter, many birds gather in large, single- or mixed-species flocks. Bosque del Apache National Wildlife Refuge is a celebrated stronghold for Ross's and Snow Geese.

Red-tailed, and Red-shouldered Hawks; and Golden Eagles all engage in aerial displays that may begin as early as late January in some parts of their ranges. Some game bird species, most notably sage grouse, Sharp-tailed Grouse, and prairie chickens, gather at leks, where multiple males display and females judge from the sidelines.

Birders can wear out a lot of shoe leather trying to walk up a Lesser Prairie Chicken in the Shin-Oak plains of eastern New Mexico. Or they can go to a lek and watch a dozen or more males dance and cavort.

Summer (May through July/August)

In summer, the situation is very different. Most species across most of North America spread out and establish territories that may be as small as a suburban yard or, as is sometimes the case with Golden Eagles, cover more than two hundred square miles. Point is, they are basically confined to their territories. Know a bird's breeding range, recognize its preferred habitat, and the actual location of the bird is almost an afterthought.

In fact, territorial birds even help you locate them. As mentioned earlier, during the breeding season, most male birds broadcast their location by vocalizing, and many are, at this time, garbed in their eye-catching best, their "breeding plumage." Every morning and most evenings (and even off and on throughout the day, particularly early in the breeding season), songbirds sing rings around their territories.

OK, woodpeckers tap out a territorial tattoo, and other birds, particularly raptors, engage in aerial displays to post notice of ownership, but the point is that during the breeding season, male birds, by and large, go out of their way to be seen or heard.

It's not vanity. It's business. Serious get-your-genes-in-the-pool business.

Most females are different. As the parent largely responsible for keeping the genetic dowry safe from harm, females are mostly reticent during the breeding season (and responsible birders respect this).

Another good thing about territoriality is that not only is it geographically limiting, its directed focus is, too. A male Blue Grosbeak

During nesting season, female birds generally try to not draw attention to themselves. This incubating Plumbeous Vireo wants nothing more than to be inconspicuous.

would be very touchy about another male Blue Grosbeak in its territory (and near its mate). But this same grosbeak is next to indifferent about the Mourning Dove, White-eyed Vireo, Yellow-breasted Chat, and Field Sparrow nesting nearby. Find one and you stand a good chance of running into other species that occupy the same range and have the same habitat requirements.

Spring and Fall Migration

The winter and summer pattern of birds is *dynamic* in that birds will be actively engaged in their seasonally calibrated pursuits but *static* in that the numbers and variety of species changes little day by day. The same birds do pretty much the same thing every day.

Spring and autumn are different. During these seasons of transition, many birds are engaged in a great geographic relocation—moving to and from breeding and wintering territories. Some, such as the tundra race of the Peregrine Falcon and many arctic-breeding shorebird species, migrate great distances, vaulting hemispheres. Other species embark on shorter journeys. Red-throated Loons, for example, abandon their breeding areas in the arctic and relocate to the Atlantic and Pacific coasts of North America as well as the Gulf of Mexico. Mountain Bluebirds, which breed at altitudes over five-thousand feet, relocate to lower elevations in winter. Prairie Falcons do not abandon their breeding range in winter so much as expand it, with some individuals relocating east, into the prairies, and farther south, into Mexico.

Spring and winter, when many bird populations are reapportioning themselves across the planet, are exciting times for birders. Some birds travel great distances, vaulting continents. Others, like the Mountain Bluebird, may simply descend from higher to lower elevations.

Whatever the distance or strategy, the point is that spring and fall migration are exciting times for bird-watchers. Every day dawns with new possibilities. With every passing weather system, nature shuffles the deck, dealing birders a new hand to play.

Just as there is rhyme and reason governing the presence and behavior of birds during the breeding and nonbreeding seasons, there are factors that influence migration, too—meteorological conditions that compel birds to move at certain times and not others, local conditions that govern where birds will be most concentrated.

Learn the rules governing bird migration and you'll play a winning hand.

First, Forget Your Notion of "Seasons"

Spring and especially fall migration are protracted. Some species begin their journeys early, some late. In spring, some very early migrants actually begin migrating while other species are still settling into their winter pattern.

How early is early? Across more temperate regions of North America (where most of the human population is found), some ducks are already heading north as early as late January. Many of these early migrants winter just below the freeze line. As open water becomes available, birds like Ring-necked Duck and Common Merganser head north to exploit it.

Want to see them? Just find open water.

Purple Martins, which winter in South America, return to Florida by early February (even late January). American Crows, Turkey Vultures, and Golden Eagles are also heading north in February, and by month's end they will be joined by bluebirds and even some swallows.

The northbound surge of birds gains in species and number in March, peaks in April and May, and continues, particularly in far northern regions, into June! This is just in time to overlap with the first of the southbound Arctic shorebird species whose brief breeding season is ending. Some postbreeding Short-billed Dowitchers and Lesser Yellowlegs are already heading south on, or shortly after, the solstice.

Yes, the summer solstice. June 21.

By early July, marshes and wetlands across the country are teeming with southbound shorebirds. Other early fall migrants, like swallows and waterfowl, are gathering in postbreeding aggregations, where they find an abundance of food (and, in the case of molting waterfowl, privacy). By late July, some songbird breeders are filtering south. In August, the trickle becomes a flood, and from then until early November, fall bird migration will sweep across

Spring and fall migrations are protracted. In spring, Purple Martins reach Florida as early as January. In autumn, the first southbound Short-billed Dowitchers leave the Arctic and reach coastal wetlands in the lower states as early as June 21.

North America, diminishing quickly but continuing, for some species (such as winter finches) into December, January, and even, in the case of irruptive species like Common Redpoll, February!

What most people think of as "spring" and "fall" migration is just "rush hour" on the great pan-hemispheric highway: April and May, late August through mid-October.

If you are interested in knowing the annual cycle of North America's breeding birds (and other facets of birds' lives), a great resource is the Cornell Laboratory of Ornithology's *Birds of North America* series. Subscriptions are available online. Contact: www.bna.birds.cornell.edu/bna or call 1-800-843-2473.

About those Conditions

As noted, different species follow different migratory timetables—dependable periods when they begin and end their journey. But even within a single species, not everybody goes at once. In some species, such as southbound shorebirds, adults precede young. In others, such as birds of prey, juveniles mostly migrate before their parents. In spring, breeding birds jump the gun on second-year birds that may (but probably won't) breed, but do, for the most part, migrate north.

The actual onset of migration commonly occurs when some biological trigger gets pulled, and this trigger is generally related to weather. In spring, most northbound birds advance on a warm front—a weather condition characterized by warming temperatures and southerly winds.

Birds, as energy-conscious creatures, like a tailwind and generally avoid migrating into energy-sapping headwinds.

In fall, the situation is reversed. It's cold fronts, associated with cold air bulging out of the north and characterized by northerly winds, that spur migration and ferry birds across the miles.

You can see these weather patterns depicted on the Weather Channel or by going online and studying the maps created by the National Weather Service. You can also, at certain times and/or locations, actually "see" birds migrating from the comfort of your recliner.

You can see them on weather radar.

Virtual Birds, TV Birding

It was Dr. Sid Gauthreaux of Clemson University who got the idea of using radar to monitor birds. Radar was developed by the British at the onset of World War II to detect incoming German air raids, and almost from the moment this new technology was put into practice, radar operators were plagued with phantom images appearing on their radar screens—"angels," as they were called.

It took a while to figure out that what the radar was picking up were birds, massed enough to send back a radar echo strong enough to be picked up by radar. It took another forty or so years before Dr. Gauthreaux, searching for some way to measure changing bird populations, realized that U.S. radar stations pointing south into the Gulf of Mexico offered a perfect historic data set.

By comparing the volume of stored images of birds migrating across the Gulf of Mexico in spring with images today, he could calculate how North America's songbird populations have diminished over time.

The technology was amazing, the results shocking. Dr. Gauthreaux calculated that a fifty percent reduction in cross-Gulf migration had transpired (and for many species, the attrition continues today).

Not the point. The fact is that at times and places birds still migrate in numbers large enough to be detected by Doppler radar—the same Doppler radar that is used to show rain and snowfall patterns on the local broadcast of the Weather Channel (offered six times an hour, "on the eights") as well as on your local daily news broadcasts.

You've probably seen these "angel" images yourself but didn't recognize that the big green flashes surrounding ground radar sites or large green lines concentrated along coastlines or river valleys or at the tips of peninsulas or along the front range were, in fact, birds!

Migrating mostly at night! Showing up on your screen most commonly in the hours after midnight and before sunrise or just after sunset (when many birds resume their migration). You'd see the big green flash on the screen (on a day that was predicted to be beautiful and clear). Step outside. Stare up into a perfectly cloudless morning sky. Shake your head.

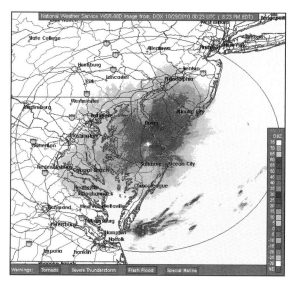

Many birds migrate at night, and large masses of birds are picked up on National Weather Radar. Pictured here is the radar echo of hundreds of thousands (if not millions) of birds over Delaware Bay at 8:23 P.M. on October 28, 2010.

IMAGE COURTESY OF THE NATIONAL WEATHER SERVICE

Now you'll know to grab your binoculars and head for your local birding patch or the nearest migrant trap.

Sometimes the people on the Weather Channel even sanctify the migratory phenomenon with a disclaimer. One September afternoon, the weatherman warned viewers that all the green showing up on the screen north of Corpus Christi, Texas, wasn't a downpour but migrating hawks.

He didn't identify them by species. But according to the migratory timetable and flocking behavior, they were undoubtedly Broad-winged and Swainson's Hawks (and maybe the odd Mississippi Kite), and they numbered in the tens of thousands.

Are birds visible everywhere on radar? Sure. Provided you have enough birds. It's just that some places are better at concentrating birds than others. Just as weather has a way of moving birds, geography has a way of directing and concentrating them, too.

To see real-time radar images on your computer, go to www.rap.ucar.edu/weather/radar or www.wunderground.com/radar/map.asp. If you live in the Northeast and are interested in an analysis of the overnight migration as captured on radar, go to www.woodcreeper.com.

The Iron Law of Leading Lines

Earlier I said that birds are not evenly distributed across the planet. This inequity applies to migration, too. While birds do have a tendency to migrate across a broad front, topographic features channel and concentrate the flow along "migratory leading lines."

In spring, for example, the Rocky Mountains constitute a barrier to migration. Because it requires energy to fly over them, and because spring is more advanced, and foraging opportunities greater at lower elevations, many northbound bird species gang up along the front range rather than challenge the snow-covered peaks.

The south shores of the Great Lakes are another concentrating mechanism. Many northbound migrants hit the south shore of Lake Erie and "fall out," opting to spend a day resting and feeding before making the jump across open water. Those birds that do make the crossing commonly head for the first piece of dry real estate they see. One very famous rest stop is called Pt. Pelee National Park, in Canada. This southward-projecting Lake Erie peninsula is a magnet for spring migrants that, after a night's migration, are searching for a dry perch in an otherwise wet stretch of planet.

The Dry Tortugas, Florida; the gulf coast from Texas to the Florida Panhandle; Cape May, New Jersey . . . all are excellent examples of coastal migrant traps.

How many birds might be expected to be found in such a migratory hot spot during prime migration? The safe answer is: considerably more than would be encountered at points along the migration route that are not geomagnified.

The enticing answer is: (at times) millions and millions. Stupendous spring migratory fallouts commonly have a meteorological as well as a geographic component. What happens, in some cases, is that a big migratory push, ferried north on the southerly or southwesterly winds of a warm front, run into or are overrun by a cold front. Hitting headwinds, and often bad weather at the edge of the front, the birds "fall out." If the cold front catches migrants over water (like the Gulf of Mexico), the weary birds are in a fight for their lives. Those that survive reach places like High Island, Texas, or Dauphin Island, Alabama, completely exhausted.

It's a birder's dream and a migrant's nightmare.

In fall, the northwest winds that trigger migration also concentrate birds along coastlines where, following the coast south, they get channeled into cul-de-sacs. Cape May, New Jersey, and Cape Charles, Virginia, are celebrated migrant traps, catching and funneling southbound migrants. Block Island, just off the coast of Rhode Island, is another magnet for waifs whose migratory ambitions were greater than the strength of their wings—which is understandable. Most of the birds migrating in fall are juveniles. Kids! Birds that have never migrated before so have no clear understanding of what they will find or face.

Like you, when you had just started birding. All they have is a genetic blueprint handed down to them from long lines of survivors. Ancestors that made this migratory jump and survived.

Another concentrating mechanism worth noting is a mountain ridge. Those running variously north-south are used as "migratory leading lines" by migrating birds of prey. Given the right winds, the updrafts off these elevated rail lines offer migrating hawks, eagles, and vultures mile upon mile of energy-conserving lift.

Hawk Mountain Sanctuary, located astride the famous Kittatinny Ridge in eastern Pennsylvania, is perhaps the most famous of these ridge sites, but others exist. And birds of prey are not the only birds attracted to mountain highways: the Appalachians constitute a corridor for many neotropical songbird migrants heading to northern breeding grounds after a winter in Central or South America.

"But," you may be thinking, "this is great if you happen to live near one of these migrant traps. But what if you don't?"

Here's my advice. Think globally and bird locally. Migrant traps don't have to be world-famous to be effective. Or, for that matter, far from people. Lots of people.

Subway Fallout

It was Memorial Day weekend, and I was visiting a friend who lived in the Bronx—a place whose name is, in the minds of most readers, the very antithesis of a birding hot spot. Be that as it may, New York City is situated right at the junction of the Middle Atlantic and New England states. Every spring and fall, millions of birds heading to and from New England and northeastern Canada pass over the lights of the city. Not a few stop by for a visit, and sometimes, given the right conditions, considerably more than a few.

Memorial Day is pushing the envelope for spring migration. By this date, most northern breeders have passed through the lower forty-eight and are setting up house in the boreal forests of Canada—one of the planet's greatest bird hatcheries. And it had been a pretty mediocre spring for migrants. Few warm fronts, a dearth of fallouts. It was fixing to go down in the record books as the spring without birds and would have—except that on that particular Memorial Day weekend, the northeastern U.S. was treated to a door buster of a fallout resulting when a flood of backed-up migrants hitched a ride north on a big push of warm southerly air only to get squeezed to, then off, the Atlantic coast by a fast-moving cold front barreling out of Canada.

Did I say a "door buster" of a fallout? Make that "epic."

At dawn, I stepped onto the small, outside balcony of my friend's fifth-floor apartment—and found two second-year male American Redstarts foraging amid the branches of an artificial tree. Later, all the way on the other end of town, we joined a group of birders from the New York City Audubon Society in the parking lot of Jamaica Bay National Wildlife Refuge. If you've ever flown in or out of Kennedy International Airport, you've flown over Jamaica Bay.

The event was billed as a bird "walk." It quickly morphed into a bird stand as participants gathered in a defensive clot, trying to come to grips with the almost incomprehensible scene around us.

I'm speaking about birds. Thousands of them. Warblers, vireos, orioles, tanagers, flycatchers of every stripe and hue. On the ground, saturating the bushes, and overhead. The place was simply crawling with migrating songbirds—mostly females and second-year males (birds that ride spring's migratory caboose).

On the bird-sighting sheet, a book whose entries are commonly listed species by species, one overjoyed and overwhelmed patron had summarized the event by writing in big block letters across two open pages: THIS IS IT!

And so it was, one of the greatest migratory fallouts I've ever witnessed (and one that actually extended from southern New England all the way to Cape Charles).

I don't remember how many species we tallied that morning. Something over 120, as best as I recall. I was told later that we'd tied the one-day record for most birds seen at Jamaica Bay (and we stopped at noon). For my part, I was just happy to have witnessed it. An epic fallout within a subway token's reach of about eleven million people. A fallout for the record books.

The Trap Next Door

With or without subway service, there is a migrant trap near you. A copse of trees on a lakeshore. A riparian corridor snaking through a bustling city. The undeveloped woodlands flanking a suburban neighborhood. The mature trees lining a street of a prairie town.

One of the finest migratory hot spots I know is a place called Crow Valley—a BLM campground nestled in a stand of Cottonwoods and Siberian Elms surrounded by tens of thousands of acres of open short-grass prairie. To woodland birds flying over this sea of grass, Crow Valley represents an island of sanctuary—one of the very few deciduous shows in town.

Crow Valley is about an hour east of Fort Collins, Colorado (and within walking distance of Briggsdale, where the miniseries *Centennial* was filmed).

Another favorite hole-in-the-wall migrant trap is a place called Butterbredt Spring, an isolated stand of Cottonwoods located in Kern County, California, on the northern end of the Mojave Desert. When you are talking Mojave, you are talking about one of the most inhospitable stretches of habitat on the planet. And yet, on any given morning in April and May, dozens, scores, even hundreds of birds materialize out the parched blue sky and descend into this spring-fed sanctuary of trees. Warblers, vireos, orioles, grosbeaks, and tanagers, not to mention the Mountain Quail that seem to be calling from every boulder and Joshua Tree.

If birds are migrating over the inhospitable likes of the Mojave Desert, be assured they are flying over your house, too. All you have to do is locate a place near you where they find the requirements all migrating birds need: shelter, food, and a little peace and quiet.

California's Butterbredt Spring, lying on the northern end of the Mojave Desert, is a celebrated spring migrant trap. If migrating birds are flying over the Mojave to get there, be assured they are also flying over your home, too, wherever that may be.

Another celebrated migrant trap—and one, perhaps, more akin to the place you live—is Garret Mountain, New Jersey. It is a natural bottleneck insofar as it lies atop the forested Watchung Ridge—an ancient geological landform rising 520 feet above the Newark Basin. But the attractiveness of Garret Mountain has been enhanced by urbanization to the east and suburbanization to the west. Migrating birds, flying over northern New Jersey, see the ridge as a verdant strip of habitat bracketed by less productive options and follow it north . . . until the ridge runs smack into Paterson, New Jersey, which is, from the standpoint of a bird looking for a place to rest and feed, a very unattractive prospect.

In fact, from the bird's standpoint, Paterson must seem about as welcoming as Mordor.

Birds respond to this urban barrier by bailing out of the sky and packing into the mature woodlands that dominate Garret Mountain County Park, just thirteen miles west of New York City and less than one mile off Exit 56A on I-80.

Picture this: You are a weary woodland migrant, and you've been flying all night. These are your choices—the nearby trees or whatever the heck all that is beyond them. Where are you going to go?

Oh, What a Beautiful Morning Flight

During migration (especially fall migration) there is a period of geographic relocation that ensues from sunrise to about mid-morning. During this time frame, many songbird species that commonly migrate at night—most notably, kingbirds, nuthatches, vireos, kinglets, warblers, tanagers, orioles, grosbeaks, and finches—fly low, into the wind, often heading in the direction opposed to their seasonal migratory path (i.e., heading north in fall instead of south).

"Morning flight" is most evident at coastal locations (and may, at key concentration points, involve tens of thousands of birds). But it is also seen along mountain ridges and, perhaps, elsewhere—riparian corridors flanked by extensive agricultural or urban areas, for example.

Morning flight may represent an effort on the part of birds to get back on their proper migratory track or find suitable habitat to spend the day in. Whatever the reason, birders who position themselves where the migrants are passing can see more birds in a morning than they might over the course of an entire season.

Of course, you still need to identify them.

Raising a Ruckus

This might seem like an inappropriate time to raise the subject of pishing insofar as the importance of honoring a bird's need for quiet time has just been raised. But no discussion of bird finding is complete without mention of this arcane, but effective, art.

Pishing: n. the employment of onomatopoeic sounds to lure birds into view.

Many species of birds can be enticed this way. The sounds most often used mimic the scolding calls of assorted species, the squealing call of an injured bird (or animal), and the vocalizations of predators that prey upon birds (like screech-owl or Northern Pygmy-Owl).

These calls, used in concert, pique the interest and ire of birds, which respond by drawing close and adding their own voices to the ruckus, drawing even more birds into the fray (and view) and so on.

What pishing attempts to do is trigger a "mobbing action," a vocal and spirited (and perfectly natural) feathered free-for-all in which multiple birds of assorted species gather to heap verbal abuse upon a predator whose cover has been blown.

Except this time there is no predator. Only a human making a bunch of silly noises.

Does it work? Mostly yes and sometimes no. Yes for some easily pish-piqued, mostly woodland species (chickadees, titmice, nuthatches, jays, many vireos and warblers, and some sparrows). No for many other species (particularly birds of open country).

When it does work, it can seem like magic, drawing birds to within arm's length and providing open views of birds that you had no idea were even in the neighborhood.

Dozens of birds. Scores of birds. All whipped into a confrontational frenzy by a series of squeaks, squeals, sushes, stutters, toots, and warbles.

How do you learn to make these sounds? Two ways. You can go into the field, listen to the scold calls of birds, and try to imitate them. Or you can buy a book called *The Art of Pishing,* which tells you how to become a pishing expert. Even comes with an audio CD.

Who would write a book about such an arcane art? That would be me, and that would also explain why I have little interest in telling you how to become an accomplished pisher in the pages of *this* book. The publisher joins me in this regard.

One thing I will say is that pishing works extremely well on chickadees and titmice—the birds that, early on, I said were the foundation of feeding flocks and whose calls were your signal that birds are about.

So now the calls of chickadees and titmice have assumed a secondary significance. Not only do they serve as an alert mechanism, they signal that a spirited bout of pishing may be in order. The choice is yours. You can hope the birds come your way. Or you can bushwhack and try and intercept the flock. Or you can entice the flock to come to you. I'm not going to suggest which technique is "best" (waiting, intercepting, or pishing). One thing I will say is that if pishing is your choice, you then exercise a good deal of control over the location of the engagement you aspire to inspire and so gain a strategic advantage (not to mention better views). It also keeps you out of the poison ivy and away from ticks, chiggers, and run-ins with park maintenance people who will want to point out that you are not allowed off the trail.

OK, so pishing can be effective. Is it ethical?

At times, no: when birds are breeding (a stressful and taxing time for birds), or when it is very cold and birds need to feed, or when there are lots of hunting predators in the neighborhood (and birds should not be distracted), or in places where there are lots of other birders present whose right to ambience you should honor. There are also places where it is banned—most notably some migrant traps, where birds are wing-weary and birding pressure already heavy.

Some people wonder whether pishing ever constitutes a warranted intrusion into the lives of birds, and while I believe it is a good question, I also believe that the answer is yes. Were this not the case, I wouldn't be sanctioning the technique in print.

Why I believe judiciously applied pishing is an acceptable practice is the same reason why I believe pishing works at all. Whatever the biological or survival-based merits of pishing, I believe that the reason most birds respond to a mobbing action is not to address a threat but to have a little fun and excitement.

The bird equivalent of screaming "nah, nah, nah; you can't get me" into the face of the neighborhood bully—e.g., a roosting owl that, hemmed in by daylight, poses no immediate threat to anyone—and, perhaps, even tempting fate by putting themselves in a modest state of risk.

One behavioral scientist of my acquaintance explained it this way: "They're showing off."

The fact is I have never seen a mobbing bird suffer any injuries at the hand or talon or claw or fang of a predator on the receiving end of the harangue. And I find it difficult to explain why transient birds with no biological imperative directing them to confront a threat that they can fly away from will go out of their way to get into the bird equivalent of a political demonstration directed at a local tyrant.

Unless they want to.

So, you are free to pish or not. Totally up to you.

One thing I do not advocate is the use of playback recordings—playing the recorded songs of birds on their breeding territories, inciting them to confront a phony challenger. What's the difference?

With pishing, you are shouting to a general audience: "Hey. Looky here. I've cornered Bad Sir Brian the Lion without his boots on. Come on over and help me blip him on the head." (If you aren't a fan of Winnie the Pooh, you probably miss the literary reference here but still get the general idea.)

By playing a territorial song in a bird's territory, you have, in biological essence, broken down the door of a bird's home and screamed, "I'm going to steal your property and your wife," as one tour leader of my acquaintance explains it.

The stakes are a little higher with recorded playback. So is, as you might expect, the stress level they illicit.

There are times when limited, targeted playbacks are acceptable—for example, when used, judiciously, by an experienced tour leader to entice forest birds into the open for momentary views by a group (instead of putting patrons at risk and disrupting a forest environment by charging off a trail).

But in this age when iPhones are in every other birder's hand and the accent upon immediate gratification has supplanted the adage "all good things come to those who wait," I find myself increasingly anxious about the sanctity and safety of birds and cool to the use of playback recordings.

Birds Finding Birds

Pishing is a way of getting birds to attract other birds by inciting a mobbing action. But, as mentioned earlier, you can use other birds to find other birds.

Remember, way back at the beginning of this book, the discussion about the human eye? And how our eyes are packed with rod cells—the mechanisms that detect motion? Well, gifted as we are with motion detectors, the human eye isn't a patch on the detection capacity of birds.

Birds can resolve detail two to three times better than humans can. Their ability to perceive color and light is not only vastly superior but generously apportioned across the entire retina (not concentrated at the center of the eye). And owing to a superabundance of rod cells, birds are able to detect then analyze rapid movements we would perceive as a blur. Finally, where human eyes are placed forward in the head (typical of predators), the eyes of most birds are placed to the side, facilitating detection in as much as 360 degrees in some species (almost twice that of even the most peripherally gifted human).

If you feed birds in your yard, you've already seen the detection ability of birds at work.

SCENE: Hosts of feathered minions crowded around the feeder. Suddenly, a jay screams. Everybody bolts. One second, a bird-filled yard; next second, an avian vacuum.

Except for the Cooper's Hawk now perched atop your pole feeder or pinning a Mourning Dove to the ground. (Mourning Doves have a hard-to-explain tendency to freeze when everybirdy else flushes, which may explain why they find it necessary to breed just about year-round.)

People who monitor bird feeders also become attentive to less-obvious clues signaled by birds that a raptor is near. Birds crouched and motionless (when they should be feeding) or birds all packed in the protective confines of a bush are dead giveaways. After a cold night, there is only one reason energy-taxed birds are not fueling up (and while that reason might not be in your line of sight, it is in sight of your feeder).

Shorebirds and waterfowl—birds that commonly forage on open mudflats, beaches, short-grass prairie, or shallow standing water—

Heads up. Birds watch out for other birds, and they pay close attention to the skies. So when a Sandhill Crane is alert, you should be, too—for hunting Golden Eagles, for instance.

are very attentive to predatory birds. When the mass of feeding birds abruptly takes wing and flies in a tightly packed ball for the horizon, look toward the opposite horizon, in the direction the Merlin, Peregrine or Prairie Falcon, or Northern Harrier is coming.

Geese and cranes are similarly attuned to hunting eagles. When flocks are still on the ground, the proximity of eagles (and their intention) can often be gleaned by being attentive to the volume of the gabble and the number of heads raised. When the volume and intensity rises, there is a hunting bird (or coyote, perhaps) maneuvering uncomfortably close. When the flock heads for the sky, look sharp.

Gulls are also good bellwethers when it comes to larger birds of prey. Over landfills or beaches where gulls sit out the high tide, any sudden eruption of birds that climbs and does not settle quickly probably means there is an eagle or other large hunting raptor in the area.

OK, it might be a vulture (false alarm) or a particularly rambunctious and tenacious Labrador Retriever off his leash, but it's probably an eagle.

Over time, I have trained myself to be attentive to the alarm calls of birds. I can't count the number of times I've been warned of an approaching Cooper's Hawk by hearing the metallic *cheh* of a European Starling, the muffled and twangy *chr, chr* of a House Sparrow, or the angry chatter of a Tree Swallow, or heard the raspy snarl of a Purple Martin dishing out disdain upon an American Kestrel that violated colony airspace.

The scold notes of mobbing birds—chickadees, titmice, jays—have been discussed, but not in reference to their usefulness in disclosing the presence of hidden, and desirable, birds. Many, and perhaps most, of the owls I find in daylight—Northern Saw-whet Owls, Northern and Ferruginous Pygmy-Owls, Long-eared Owls, and my only Flammulated Owl—have been disclosed to me by a cloud of scolding birds.

Crows habitually, and noisily, harass roosting Great Horned Owls (Red-tailed Hawks are favorite targets, too). Gulls will go out of their way to dive on a Snowy Owl resting on a beach (and they'll be keening their displeasure as they do).

Flocks of Tree Swallows not only can signal the presence of an aerial predator, they can sometimes even aid with the identification. In summer, after the breeding season, and in winter, Tree Swallows gather in large flocks numbering, at times and in places, in the thousands. If an American Kestrel is in the area, the birds respond by coalescing around it. The location of the falcon is pinpointed by the thickened clot of birds in the sky. But if the falcon is a Merlin, a larger, faster, and more potent predator, Tree Swallows get out of the way. In a sky filled with swallows, the Merlin will be found in the spot surrounded by open air.

Starlings (and some shorebirds and blackbirds) make great bell-wethers when it comes to disclosing the presence of very distant birds of prey—hawks too distant to be picked up with the naked eye. When a Sharp-shinned Hawk enters starling airspace, the flock responds by taking wing and massing in a tight ball that wheels and maneuvers *over* the intruder. At a distance, these dancing birds appear as a dark puff of smoke in the sky that appears and disappears as the birds turn and wheel. Find the puff. Look below. Find the hawk.

Speaking of hawks, birds of prey, whose eyes are especially keen, are very helpful when it comes to finding other birds of prey. If a perched Red-tailed Hawk cocks its head and peers up or if a Peregrine Falcon on a nest ledge begins bobbing its head while gazing toward the horizon, look sharp and follow its gaze. There's another bird in the area.

Sometimes the absence of birds can be just as telling as their presence. In winter, in northern coastal areas, foraging gulls space themselves fairly evenly along beaches, each bird patrolling (and defending) its territory. If you find a stretch of beach that is curiously gull free, start scanning the upper beach, paying particular attention to elevated points—dunes or drifted logs or derelict boats that appear to have a Clorox bottle perched on top.

Clorox bottles rarely perch on derelict boats. But in areas where they are found, Snowy Owls do so habitually.

Hiding in Plain View: Big Oceans, Trackless Skies, One of the Crowd

Bird watching is not just popular, it is specialized. Some groups of birds attract the focus of ardent fans and, owing to the habitats they frequent (open air and open seas, for example) detection brings its own special challenges. In addition, and just as birds are not evenly apportioned across the planet, some species are simply less common than others. There is a tendency for uncommon and, from a birding standpoint, very desirable species to associate with similar species—offering both opportunities and challenges.

Hawk Watching—Vaulting the Distance

Broadly speaking, the animal kingdom is divided into two subgroups: predators and prey. The line between them is not absolute (in fact, most birds both consume other living things and are themselves prey to other, larger animals).

Example: Robin. It eats earthworms and is eaten by Cooper's Hawks.

But one of the basic tenets of biology is that predators must be less common than their prey or else they'd starve. Birds of prey,

North America has a number of celebrated hawk-watching junctions. The Gunsight Mountain Hawk Count, conducted about two hours' drive from Anchorage, doesn't get big crowds, but it does get lots of migrating raptors from late March to early May.

which rank among the animals that lie at, or close to, the top of the food pyramid, are least common of all. In summer and winter, when birds of prey maintain large territories, they can be very few and far between.

But migration is sort of a biological bottleneck. There are times, places, and conditions when it is possible to see a great many raptors of different species from a single spot, and in a single day.

How many species? A dozen or more. How many individuals? Hundreds, thousands, even tens of thousands.

Location, Location, Location. Remember the discussion about migratory bottlenecks and leading lines? Well, migrating hawks are concentrated along leading lines like mountain ridges and coastlines. Many of these—Hawk Mountain; Hawk Ridge in Duluth, Minnesota; Corpus Christi, Texas; the Golden Gate Hawk Watch in San Francisco; and, especially, Veracruz, Mexico—are celebrated autumn concentration points. In spring, the Rio Grande Valley of Texas; Whitefish Point, Michigan; and Rochester, New York, catch the northbound flight. (There are hundreds of other hawk-watch points and many yet to be discovered. To find a site near you, go to www.hmana.org/sitesel.php.)

Hawk-watching Basics. You will need binoculars, because hawk watching is a discipline that involves hours of scanning. A spotting scope, fitted to a tripod or on a shoulder mount, is also handy—to aid with distant identifications and enjoy birds that may never get very close.

One thing you won't have to do is get up in the dark. Hawks, whose migration, for most species, is tied closely to thermal lift, don't commonly migrate before thermals begin to develop (so not before nine A.M.), and their migration often tapers off by late afternoon.

Early (and late) in the day, use binoculars to scan the horizon. Panning smoothly, turning mostly from the waist, search the sky and the land above (and below) the horizon, covering an area just short of 180 degrees (i.e., the world in front of you). By keeping the horizon in your binoculars, you can gauge the speed of your sweep. You need to pan slowly so your eyes will be able to latch onto a distant bird of prey before your binocular field passes on.

You will, in most cases, be looking for a very, very small target: "speck birds," as my wife calls them.

Between scans, keep your eyes open for hawks that suddenly materialize, from below if you are on a mountain ridge, or from thin air as small, ground-hugging hawks pop up and speed by.

Remember, you are at a known hawk-watch junction. A place where these birds are known to pass. Be patient. When you (or other observers) find a hawk, note what it does. How and where hawks fly on any given day has a great deal to do with wind direction and prevailing conditions. What one hawk does others are likely to do, too. Once you establish the pattern, or flight path, you can better concentrate your search efforts.

In less than half an hour after hawks first start soaring, you'll probably need to scan higher. Waxing thermals mean higher-flying hawks. A good technique is to continue to make the low scan along the horizon then, when you reach the end of your sweep, raise your binoculars one binocular field above the approximate top of your initial scan. Map another search of the sky, working back along the path you came by (only higher).

Two sweeps is generally enough to cover the sky (three at the most). Later, as birds get higher, you'll need to pay more attention to the sky directly overhead. High-flying birds are difficult to detect, their presence masked by distance. But when birds are directly overhead, they show the maximum surface area. This is the point you are most likely to see them—either with your naked eye or binoculars.

A couple of tricks: Try scanning the base of clouds. Not only are hawks silhouetted against the backdrop but hawks are drawn to cumulus clouds (which are the visible, terminal stage of a thermal, the bubbles of warm air hawks seek to gain altitude).

Large, dark birds (like vultures) are much easier to find than most hawks, which are usually much paler, smaller, and melt into the sky. But hawks and vultures both use thermals, and they don't mind sharing. If you find a high-flying vulture, scan the airspace around it for other birds.

When you do find a hawk gliding past, try moving your binocular ahead three or four binocular fields to see if there is a bird ahead of it. Finding none, go back and pick up your original bird then track back three or four binocular fields to see if your initial bird has a caboose.

Many birds of prey (including many buteos, harriers, eagles, kestrels, and osprey) travel in pairs and small, well-spaced groups (up to eight or ten individuals at some exceptional sites and under good migratory conditions). Those that travel in large aggregations (Broad-winged and Swainson's Hawks and Mississippi Kites) make their presence known by clustering in "kettles" or "boils" when a stream of migrants intersects a thermal and the stream of birds clusters and swirls as they ride the elevator aloft. It was these "kettles" that the Weather Channel radar was picking up in Texas (and they can be noted elsewhere, too).

The conditions that precipitate songbird moment also spur migrating hawks—cold fronts and north-to-northwest winds in the fall; warm fronts and southerly winds in the spring. But local geography imparts a regional twist. On mountain ridges, a cloudy sky may mean even better movement (since hawks, deprived of thermals, will be dependent upon updrafts associated with the ridge). At other places, such as coastal peninsulas, heavy, overcast conditions dampen the flight.

One last point regarding weather: in spring, an approaching cold front often creates a temporary leading line. Hawks (and other soaring birds) will use the strong southwesterly winds in advance of the front to migrate, and the approaching wall of clouds constitutes a barrier. An hour (or so) before the front passes, some great hawk watching can be had by monitoring movement ahead of this impromptu leading line. When it passes, the show is over.

Spring hawk migration begins in February and extends into June, with peaks for most species and at most locations occurring from late February into mid-May. In fall, migrating hawks may pass as early as late July, and migration may continue into December and even January. But most raptors pass between late August and mid-November.

Late in the season, if snow blankets northern areas, birds of prey often respond by heading farther south.

Then there are birds such as immature Bald Eagles that wander widely for the first three or four years of their lives. They can turn up any time.

Birding the High Seas

Given our species' penchant for expression and long linguistic history, there are very few thoughts that have not been forged into words. But I'm fairly certain this is one:

"Look, dear, there's a White-faced Storm-Petrel on the birdbath."

My confidence is bolstered by the understanding that White-faced Storm-Petrels are, relative to many pelagic species, uncommon. That they are, as a bird that spends most of its life at sea, saltwater obligates (and most birdbaths contain fresh water). Perhaps most important, the only time these small, fairylike seabirds come ashore is to breed.

And that the closest island hosting a White-faced Storm-Petrel colony barely lies within ballistic missile range of North American birders.

Yet the birds regularly occur off the Atlantic coast in late summer. White-faced Storm Petrel is just one of many birds specialized to thrive in the marine environment. Along both coasts (and the Gulf of Mexico), the waters above the continental shelf support a wealth of seabirds—shearwaters, petrels, and albatrosses (mostly along the west coast), as well as other bird groups. All you have to do is get there. That's the challenge—or one of the challenges, anyway.

Most of the species encountered during a pelagic birding trip are unlikely to be seen on or even from land. I'm not certain what's being pointed out on this trip off Monterey, California (top), but it's a good bet that a Sooty Shearwater is nearby.

For reasons that will be discussed, locating birds in a habitat devoid of trees, bushes, boulders, and other obstacles can be surprisingly challenging—but well worth the effort.

Getting There. The problem of finding pelagic birds has been considerably reduced, or, more accurately, the problem has been deferred. Along both coasts, there are birding guides who specialize in organizing and leading pelagic birding trips. Depending upon the proximity of birds to the dock, trips may leave in the morning and return in the afternoon. Other trips, traveling farther offshore, may depart the evening of one day and return late the next. Multiple-day trips, for species found a hundred or more miles offshore, are also offered.

Pelagic birding hot spots include the waters off Cape Hatteras, North Carolina, and Monterey Bay, California, as well as off

Massachusetts, Maine, Washington, New Jersey, Delaware, and elsewhere. To learn about trips being scheduled out of these and other locations, search for "pelagic birding trips" online. Three websites worth checking out are www.patteson.com, www.shearwaterjourneys.com, and www.paulagics.com.

As with land-based species, there is a seasonality to the movements of seabirds and specificity with regard to habitat. It may look uniform, but be assured the marine environment is as complex and differentiated as any other. Water temperature is a determining factor. So is sea depth, salinity, and, of course, the presence (or absence) of food.

It's the job of pelagic trip organizers to know when and where to look. Your job, once you sign on for one or more trips, is to know *how* to look. Remember that if you are traveling a considerable distance, you might want to book more than one trip. Pelagic trips get weathered out fairly often.

Getting Strategic. For a successful pelagic trip, you will need binoculars, and they should be waterproof. Even if you are careful and your binoculars don't take a wave, they may still fog internally in the moisture-rich air. You should also bring a supply of cleaning cloths to wipe your lenses of salt spray. (My technique: Lick and wipe. You'll taste when the lens is clean.)

A boat is a study in applied ambivalence. Yes, it gets you where you want to go. But it does so at a price. First, as a platform from which to get a look at birds, boats are rarely stable. Also, and with amazing frequency, they are right in your way.

Consider that there are four sides to every boat: bow, stern, starboard, and port. No matter where you stand, there will be times when it is in exactly the wrong spot—i.e., the boat you are standing on stands between you and the bird you want to see.

So, too, will be a host of other birders who, like you, chose the wrong place in this particular instance.

Many birders like to position themselves in the bow, particularly when boats are under way. In the bow, you stand the best chance of seeing resting birds that the boat kicks off the water. Also, birds swinging in to take a look at your boat but have no intention of lingering often pass in front of the bow and keep going.

The bow is also generally the most bouncy place to be and, very often, the wettest. If you are prone to seasickness, be elsewhere. If seas are rough and you take a wave, you'll either be very happy you have waterproof binoculars or very upset that you do not. Either way, you'll be wet.

The stern, particularly on pelagic trips where chum is tossed overboard to lay down a bird-attracting oil slick, can also be productive—because of the bait, and because some species of pelagic birds are "ship followers" that commonly come up on a ship in the wake.

The sides midship are generally the most stable locations on a boat (i.e., subject to less rise and fall than the bow and stern), but, from the standpoint of "getting on" birds, they are also often the least productive. There are 360 degrees worth of ocean out there, and your view from the side is limited to about half.

Still, the port or starboard sides might be the best bet. Pelagic birds drawn to chum slicks do tend to remain in view, and captains do maneuver so that all people on board get views (time and situation providing). In the morning, standing on the side of the boat facing away from the sun will kill the glare and make it easier to find birds. If there are rough seas, standing on the leeside of the boat will keep you and your binoculars dry. Birders on the windward side will have to contend with waves and spray.

If the boat has an upper deck accessible to passengers, this is, arguably, the best place to stand. On the upper deck, only the bow is blocked (by the cabin's superstructure) and you are, except in unusually bad seas, above the spray zone.

But if you are prone to seasickness, stay away from the upper deck. In this case, what you want, and trust me on this, is a place by the rail—the lower rail. Hurling from the upper deck is not going to win you any friends, and it may cost you the ones you have.

Scanning. Pelagic birding is a lot like hawk watching in that you both scan with your binoculars and keep your eyes alert for birds that suddenly appear (which, surprisingly, they do).

Keep your feet spaced apart and lean up against something—the rail or bulkhead. This will give you three anchoring points. If the engine is running, try keeping your knees loose. The articulation of bone to bone will transmit the vibration from the deck right to your binoculars, reducing image quality. If you unlock the joints in your knees, part of the engine vibration will be absorbed by the muscles in your legs.

Scan the horizon for birds that commonly pop into view then disappear, dropping into concealing troughs. Gauge the bird's speed. Anticipate where it is going to reappear then pan your binoculars, slowly, back and forth over that spot.

Many seabirds, most notably shearwaters, fly just above the surface, and many use waves the way hawks use ridges, to gain energy and lift. Some species, such as albatrosses, bound over the ocean, rising and falling like slow-motion skipped stones (actually, in high winds, many seabirds, including gannets, shearwaters, and jaegers, have a bounding flight). Storm-petrels patter and dance or zigzag across the surface. Alcids and phalaropes tend to sit on the water in small groups and, when flushed, head away from the boat.

Skuas, tropicbirds, and kittiwakes commonly appear high in the air above the boat (and often suddenly). In migration, small groups of Long-tailed Jaegers will fly 100 to 150 feet above the surface, rarely showing an interest in ships.

There will be lots of eyes on board, many of them experienced. The key to pelagic birding is staying on deck and being in position to get on birds that may be distant and may not linger. The key to staying on deck is staying warm and dry; this means good outerwear. The key to being in position often boils down to outlasting everybody else on board then maneuvering to take the best spot.

Just like land birds, pelagic birds have different feeding strategies and flight styles. Some species patter across the water, some fly high and direct, and some, such as albatross, bound across the ocean in looping arches.

Birds of a Feather, Not

There is a lot of truth to the old cliche "birds of a feather flock together." Equally true is the tendency of less common but closely related species to team up with their more common brethren.

Your job is to find them. In fact, one of birding's defining and manifest challenges lies in using your skills to find birds that are rare or outside their normal range. Aiding you in this regard are those most basic of senses discussed at the very beginning of this book—your evolved ability to home in on things that are anomalous, different, and new.

In a strictly sensory sense, finding the odd bird in a flock is no more difficult than picking out the individual that looks different. The problem is that, many times, the differences between one species and another closely related species are slight. In addition, distance, poor light conditions, and views that may be partially blocked by other birds diminish or mask what differences there might be.

But the primary reason unusual birds are missed by observers is because observers don't know to look for them and, if they do, don't know what differences to look for.

OK, now you know to look. Know that when you find a group of birds—shorebirds feeding across a mudflat, gulls loafing on a sandbar, geese packing an impoundment—the universe has just thrown down a glove. It has challenged you to pick the rare bird or birds out of the flock, the ruby or diamond tucked in among the quartz and garnets. There are two ways to approach this challenge.

Yes, birds of a feather do flock together. And similar species do, too. Sometimes finding the uncommon bird among more common confederates is easy— like picking out the Roseate Tern among these Common Terns.

I Perceive, Therefore I See

You can simply employ your innate ability to discern differences. Bigger versus smaller, lighter versus darker. You have a direct comparison: birds side by side. Let your eye be drawn. Once it locks on the target then start being critical. Is this darker (or larger or stockier or taller) bird really different?

One of the greatest identification challenges I know relates to basic-plumage Western and Semipalmated Sandpipers. In September and October, both species occur in New Jersey. Plumage differences are slight, bordering on nonexistent. Bill length varies and overlaps, and while some female Western Sandpipers are distinctly longer billed, many individuals have bill lengths in that indeterminate range.

Then I learned a trick—one aided by direct comparison. Western Sandpipers, owing in part to their larger bills, are basically more front-heavy than are Semipalmated Sandpipers. When resting side by side, semipalmateds maintain a horizontal profile. Front-heavy westerns are obliged to stand slightly more upright to balance the load more evenly on their legs.

You want to pick the westerns out of a flock of semis, look first for the ones standing ever-so-slightly taller and whose stance appears more upright.

Several years ago, I was birding the Salton Sea with Bob Miller, a local birding expert. He was driving, I was watching, and we were traveling down a gravel road, probably thirty, forty miles per hour, passing about a hundred Ring-billed Gulls a second. The agricultural fields flanking the road were simply paved with these winsome gulls.

Something caught my eye.

"Stop," I urged. Bill did.

"Back up," I urged. Bill complied.

Finding the bird that caught my eye, I brought my binoculars up and confirmed what my eyes gleaned and what my mind had recognized as a possibility.

"Adult Mew Gull," I noted, conversationally.

"You the man!" Bill observed, just as conversationally.

Did I *identify* the bird at forty miles per hour? No. My eyes simply registered a bird that was different. Helping me in this regard was the uniform backdrop. Had the field held a mix of gull species—a mosaic of sizes, shapes, and patterns—it's unlikely that the subtle difference between Ring-billed and Mew Gull would ever have grabbed my eye. But it's not the only reason I found the bird. More on that later.

Different Begets Difference

Species differ for a reason, and the reason usually involves what they do and how they do it. Two birds that are identical would be expected to behave identically. Two birds that differ by small degrees—length of their bills, length of their legs, color of their backs—often betray these differences spatially and behaviorally.

Take Short-billed Dowitchers and Stilt Sandpipers. Both feed by wading and probing. But when foraging in the same pool, Stilt Sandpipers, owing to their longer legs, commonly forage in deeper water and so away from, or at the edge of, a flock of feeding dowitchers.

Take Little Gull, a petite gull with dark underwings that, in North America, commonly associates with the larger and much more common Bonaparte's Gull. But being smaller, Little Gulls are often picked on by Bonaparte's. While roosting "in" the flock, there is often extra space between a Little Gull and a flanking Bonaparte's. In a line of gulls, the smaller, picked-on gull, the different gull, is also often the bird at the edge of the flock, too.

This clannishness among birds is not limited to gulls. Snow Geese will sometimes drive Ross's Geese away if one of the smaller Ross's encroaches within bill length. If you see a bird being picked on by other members of a flock, look critically. If you see a bird standing slightly apart or one that seems to move about more, unable to find its place in the flock, it is worth your dedicated study.

The clannishness of birds cuts two ways. Across much of North America, the challenge on finding a flock of Lesser Scaups is to pick out the Greater Scaup in their midst. Sometimes when I find a bird that looks slightly larger, rounder headed, larger billed, whiter sided, I'll note that, in fact, it looks identical to the bird next to it.

With good reason. Birds of a feather flock together even, and maybe particularly, when they are in the minority. If there are two or more Greater Scaups in the mix, chances are they will be, in the spirit of "birds of a feather," found together. Side by side.

I Anticipate, Therefore I Find

Back to that Mew Gull. The one I picked out at forty miles an hour. Yes, part of the reason I found it was because it was simply different—different enough to catch my eye. But the other reason was because I was looking for it—I knew that finding a Mew Gull amid Ring-billed Gulls was a possibility. The difference I noted was facilitated by awareness—the foreknowledge that I should be on the lookout for a very slightly smaller, very slightly darker-backed, more elegantly proportioned gull among the ring-billeds.

I.e., I was applying a search image. All I had to do was sift and match.

If finding new and unusual birds strikes a chord in you, then you've got a lot of homework to do. You need to know that Little Gulls and Black-headed Gulls often associate with Bonaparte's Gulls. When you come upon a flock of Horned Larks, you should know that longspurs often forage with larks. If you find a flock of Lapland Longspurs, you need to know that there are three other species of longspur whose winter range is more restricted than the Lappie's but that are known to wander outside their established ranges.

When they do, they most often team up with their more widespread brethren.

How do you gain the insight I'm speaking about here? One way is to go online and see the photographs of rare birds posted on a number of websites serving the birding crowd. Often these vagrant species are posing among likely confederates. All you have to do is take note of the company vagrants keep.

Another way is to pick up a book called *Pete Dunne's Essential Field Guide Companion*. In each species account is a section entitled COHABITANTS—birds that species commonly associate or share the same habitat with.

Canada Geese, right! But look closely: See anything different? Try picking out big ones versus small ones. Knowing what to look for goes a long way toward finding what you seek, and this knowledge extends to realizing that the smaller subspecies of Canada Geese have been split off and are now regarded as a separate species: Cackling Geese. (But just because they split doesn't mean they don't still dine together.)

But by far the best way to learn how and where and with whom to associate the appearance of rare and/or highly desirable species is simply to spend lots of time in the field, gaining experience, increasing the size and scope of the cognitive net you cast at the world each time you go birding.

How do you tell a Smith's or Chestnut-collared Longspur from a Lapland? Sorry. That's an identification problem. As noted earlier, that's not within the scope of this book.

5 | Here and Now: Where the Gray Matter Meets the Challenge

Range, seasonality, weather systems, habitat specializations, social proclivities. You've learned a great deal about the factors that motivate birds to be in certain places at certain times. But in birding, as in life, the devil is often in the details. What motivates a flock of Ring-necked Ducks to be on *this* side of a lake and not *that*, or a migrant flock of warblers to be in *this* patch of woodlands and not *another*, is the nitty-gritty bottom line.

There is as much rhyme and reason to local bird occurrence and movement as there is to broad-based patterns. Much of it has to do with immediate local weather conditions, some of it with short-term phenomena that birds can exploit. A lot of it has to do with the physical layout and opportunities presented by the patch you are birding right now.

The point is that while local bird movement might be causally linked, even predictable, it is not necessarily regular or dependable.

What you need in order to effectively play the field (or woodlands, or marsh, or whatever) is the ability to read a landscape, note conditions, predict how these will affect bird distribution right here and now, and act accordingly.

A lot of it is just common sense.

Sunny Disposition

Do you remember our first walk together? The one where you found the Hermit Thrush and feeding flock of chickadees? Well, chances are you had a choice of trails or, at the very least, the option of going one way or the other.

I don't know what determined your choice, but I'm going to offer a hint now. Based on the species you found (and didn't find), I'd say we took that walk in winter. Winter mornings are generally cool, so were I planning your walk, I would have chosen a route that would intersect lots of sunlight falling on a sheltered woodland edge.

My choice isn't based on personal comfort. It is predicated upon an understanding that birds like to warm up on cool mornings as much as people do. Also, protected, sunny places are where insect activity is going to be the greatest the earliest.

On cool mornings in autumn, winter, and spring, bird the sunny edge. Conversely, in summer, when birds are overheating in the middle of the day, seek out cooler, shady places near water.

There is another advantage to birding the sunny edge. The sun will be at your back, making viewing easier.

Wind

It's a lament so often expressed in birding circles that it approaches the level of a cliche: "I'd much rather bird in the rain than the wind."

Both conditions can be challenging. But both can be productive, too. While a world set in motion by wind does detract from our ability to detect birds and mask our ability to hear them, wind also directs and concentrates birds, making them, in many cases, easier to locate.

Not surprisingly, most birds share our antipathy toward wind. It makes it harder to detect predators. It robs them of heat. It makes it difficult to fly or swim except in one direction (and for ducks on open water, it means having to relocate over and over again because they are constantly being blown out of position).

When it's windy, birds (and birders) seek shelter. The lee side of woods or hedges. Just over the lip of a hill or in a sheltered ravine. The calm windward side of the lake or marsh.

When it's blowing a gale, don't even bother to scan the side of a pond being pounded by waves. All the birds are going to be snug up against the shore of the windward side (and many birds will be tucked in the vegetation, where it is the calmest).

Songbirds, particularly insect-eating songbirds, seek out protected pockets to forage (and not just birds that search for insects among the leaves). On multiple occasions, I've enjoyed the sight of hundreds of swallows sweeping insects out of the air along sheltered woodland edges. The birds are concentrated where flying insects aren't getting their wings blown off. These wind-driven concentrations hold another advantage. Birds are reluctant to leave them. You can stand amid feeding swallow flocks and the birds will as good as ignore you, passing at arm's length.

The same goes for birds on the ground. Feeding pipits, sparrows, and longspurs will commonly allow closer approach than they would if winds were light. Consider: They are already precisely where they want to be. Flush them and there is only one energetically efficient way to retreat—with the wind. If they want to return to that favored patch of ground, they are going to have to fly into a headwind to get there. Rather than deal with this, they stand their ground, gambling that you'll pass them by or stop short. Which, of course, given your interest in studying them, you will.

A word about using optics in the wind. To reduce image-compromising vibration, try standing behind some blocking object (like your car) and leaning your elbows on the roof or hood. When using a spotting scope, try not extending the legs; use the hood of your car for support. Even a subcompact car weighing 2,500 pounds is much less shaky than a six-pound tripod.

Storms

If weather deals birders a new hand, storms really shuffle the deck. Normal bird patterns are disrupted. There is a great deal of relocation in the wake of storms.

Along the east and gulf coasts, birders and surfers are probably the only people who pray for hurricanes. These large systems spawned in tropical seas trap birds in the calm eye of the storm and ferry them well north of their normal ranges. Where the eye passes, exotic birds magically appear on coasts and inland bodies of water (often well inland—like the Great Lakes). Also, coastal (and inland areas) falling mostly east of the eye also enjoy a bird dividend when hurricanes make landfall. This is where most of the storm's waifs will be deposited.

But any strong coastal storm forces and ferries pelagic species inland—some, like Great Black-backed Gulls, seeking shelter; others, like jaegers, simply ferried by the wind.

The best jaeger experience I ever had was precipitated by a massive October storm, a nor'easter that is still talked about in Cape May. The winds blew southeast for the better part of the day, piling up water in the Delaware Bay. As the storm passed, the rain abated and the winds shifted southwest. Heading out to the westernmost jetty in Cape May Point, we were greeted by a virtual parade of Parasitic and Pomarine Jaegers. The birds had been "blown" into the bay by the easterly winds then pinned to the west side of the peninsula (the east side of the bay) as they tried to make their escape back to sea. The parade of birds was literally at our feet.

Another bird-producing force of nature is a cold front passing during spring or fall migration. The propensity of these frontal boundaries (and the stormy weather that precedes them) to concentrate migrating birds of prey along their leading edges has already been mentioned. But these walls of bad weather also prompt migrating ducks, geese, gulls, and terns to bail out of the sky.

Passing frontal boundaries often force migrating birds out of the sky. Checking large inland bodies of water after a night of rain or the passage of a cold front may produce unusual birds, perhaps even an Arctic Tern or a Red-throated Loon.

On the heels of a cold front in from March to early June, it often pays to check the nearest large body of water (a lake or reservoir) to see what may have dropped out of the sky. Scoters, Bonaparte's Gulls, Arctic Terns, and jaegers are not common fare on inland lakes, but many that do occur are storm related.

Periodic Opportunities: When Ma Nature Throws You a Bone

The bounty spawned by storms sometimes lingers—and that is just one of the impromptu opportunities that birders need to be mindful of. Strong storms often stir up the seabed, depositing clams and other mollusks along beaches. Gulls, as opportunistic scavengers, gather, and gather, and gather, leaving only when the food gives out. The more gulls you have, the greater the likelihood that an unusual one will show up.

Fish die-offs caused by oxygen depletion are also gull magnets. Spring thaw, when fish frozen in the ice become available, is another.

Summer drought concentrates fish in the shallows—and herons and egrets gather to the feast. When oaks flower in the spring, the blossoms attract nectar-feeding insects (at a time when insect numbers are low). In some parts of the country, spring warbler migration is essentially fueled (indirectly) by flowering oaks and other flowering trees.

During the 1990 World Series of Birding, our newest teammate, charged with scouting the northern part of our route, altered the itinerary to intersect what was, at first, and second glance, too, a dispirited clump of brush and trees.

"What's here?" one of my teammates asked darkly, voicing a skepticism shared by all.

What was there was just about every species of eastern warbler you could name, plus Swainson's Thrush, plus Black-billed Cuckoo. The migratory mother lode!

"Whatever made you stop here?" I asked.

"Well," said our scout, "I drove by it several times while scouting and suddenly it hit me that every time I went by, the place was filled with singing birds."

As well it should. What the wall of trees and brush was hiding was an overgrown apple orchard whose blossomed branches were alive with pollinating insects.

The important thing to realize about periodic opportunities is that while they may be irregular, even unpredictable, they also tend to be somewhat enduring. A drought that exposes lots of lakeshore during July and August is going to continue to attract migrating shorebirds as long as the water continues to recede. A patch of oak in flower that is attracting lots of feeding spring migrants will continue to host birds until the trees stop blooming. If you find a concentration of migrants feeding in the treetops on Tuesday, chances are very good there will be birds there on Friday.

And some periodic opportunities are very predictable. In fact, annual. Farmers turning their soil in the spring expose earthworms that attract more than robins. Many shorebird and heron species also forage on freshly turned ground. Farmers cutting hay send up a spray of insects that attract swallows. Engineered (or natural) grassland fires are the signal for some birds of prey to gather to the feast. The flames flush small birds and mammals. Birders traveling

Every May on the beaches of the Delaware Bay, breeding horseshoe crabs deposit eggs that attract hundreds of thousands of northbound shorebirds, including Red Knot and Ruddy Turnstone. In July, billions of brine flies attract a million migrating phalaropes to the Great Salt Lake. In March, half a million Sandhill Cranes gather on the Platte River in Nebraska. You've got your work cut out for you if you want to experience these great birding spectacles—but that's why you're a birder, right?

to the Texas coast in search of White-tailed Hawks know to be on the lookout for smoke. Where there is smoke, there are hunting white-taileds.

Every May in the Delaware Bay, hundreds of thousands of horse-shoe crabs haul up on beaches to deposit their eggs. Tens of thousands of northbound shorebirds gather to feast upon them. Every July, on the Great Salt Lake, hundreds of thousands of Red-necked and Wilson's Phalaropes gather to feast on a bounty of brine flies.

The natural world is dynamic. Feast and famine. Ebb and flow. Now you see them, now you don't.

By and by, you'll learn to anticipate periodic opportunities that cause great bird concentrations and birding opportunities. You'll make it part of your avocational wisdom and birding pattern.

For now, your challenge is to be aware. To become attuned to the natural world and develop a level of intimacy. It has often been said that the key to recognizing rare birds is to learn the common ones first. The same goes for birding opportunity. The way to recognize a condition worth exploiting is to become familiar enough with the world around you to know when it changes.

There is no better way to gain this intimacy than to go birding. And no more pleasurable way either.

Last Things Last

Any last thoughts before I let you start putting your bird-finding skills to the test? A couple. First and foremost, bear in mind that bird watching is an activity that is supposed to be fun, and the pleasure of birding is meant to last a lifetime. If birding were an avocation that could be mastered in a week, we'd all have to find another activity to engage and challenge us.

Learning about the birds that are the focus of birding is a lifelong pursuit. So enjoy it. Study the birds you find. Don't just check them off and move on to the next. Savor them. Learn from them. Gain from them.

The more you know about the birds you seek, the more birds you'll find. The more birds you find, the more you'll learn. It's what gets bird-watchers up in the morning, every morning, and . . .

It also helps explain why bird watching is North America's second-largest and fastest-growing outdoor pursuit.

Acknowledgments

I t is with special thanks that I single out several people whose talents figure in this book. First, as in everything, my wife Linda whose images grace many of these pages and Mike Hannisian whose photographic talents are also showcased here. Dr. David La Puma selected and sent on the radar image found on page 47. Bill Boyle and Karen Thompson very kindly reviewed the manuscript as did Mark Allison, editor, Stackpole Books, who is both a credit to the publishing industry and a fine person to work with. My sincere thanks, too, to Kathryn Fulton, Editorial Assistant, for her patience and for all that she did to facilitate this effort.